PREFACE

Grace and Peace to You from God our father and the Lord Jesus
Christ. The books are Very Special book, it is History book, with
sensitive information's, it will be sold very expensive Price. If
You have these book, keep it in secure way and pass on to Your
family. The Power of Productivity has a lot of information's how
the economy of the world build throughout history. It is going
saves trillions of Dollars how the Economy of the world runs,
for all government around the world. The history of Economy,
the transformations, from traditional ways of building the Life of
the world and it is Economy on to the modern ways of building,
the Life of the world which is through the government. The
transformations from exchanging goods for buying and selling on
to how the government started to create money for buying and
selling's. How to balance Economy and make it grow.? Why some
other Countries Economies is not as strong as some developed
Countries. What they have to do in order to Change their Country
and build a great economy. How to Print Money in order to,
Balance the Economy. The importance of Creativity, in Economic
development and transformations. How to transform and build the
world, through modern School systems and the new technology.

In the modern economy building, the importance of education and Global trading systems. In Economy building, through creativity and productivity, the importance of Faith into the divine Holy God and Courage into the Holy Lord. How to transform Economy and build a great economy through faith and Courage into the Holy Lord. How to build a Great economy from Scratch and transform it through industrializations. How to transform Economy without falling to the next generations. You can recommend all manufacturers , universities, and government around the world. It is going to Change everything for everyone. As You all know, in order to build a better world knowledge and leadership is very important. Leaders, transform and build the world with the knowledge they know and knowing sometimes comes through reading a great book like these. The reason I do these kinds of works, in these time and Century the world needs help and transformations to the next generations and transformations happens through knowing and doing it to build a better world.

The rest of the Chapter of the book is also History books. It is about the History of the Holy God, the God who made the heavens and the earth, the God of Jesus Christ. If You want to learn the difference between all religions, you need to spend sometimes reading these books. All in all, You guys already knows me what kinds of works I do, with all my books. I am Hoping these books will give You more knowledge, to the knowledge You already have.

In order to have these book, you don't have to be Christian only, its good if everyone has it and learn from it. It's going to Change many people Life around the world and defeated poverty.

I want to say, thank You Very Much and God Bless You.

Content's

Chapter 1

1) How government Print's money, to balance the Economy.? The answer is, Yes Government can Print money or as they always Print for their annual national budget, you can increase the amount money You Print Every Years for Your Economy. So, If You run Out of money, sometimes You can Print more money to Increase Productivity, Job Creations, strengthening trades , Sporting Educations, research Intuitions in order to Grow Productivity to transform the Economy and Build it.

These terms my not be good for the third world countries. They can still Print more money and they have to know where they have to spend their money in order to increase Productivity and tread. They cannot Print their money and buy foreign exchange in order to buy Product. But, they can increase Printing their own money and spend, on their Own Manufacture, in order to increase Productivity and trades, so through trades they can build the Economy, without weakness their money value. These can strengthen their Economy and build it. They can also spend on Educations, research intuitions, things like that, in order to increase Productivity and Job Creations.

2) The Key thing is How to Increase Productivity, creativity, and trades, without losing Quality. How to transform, the world Economy with the New technology.? The world has to learn how

to create and transform all things together, in order to build the world and its Economy. As, I said, in these all Faith and Courage play big role to make all things work.

3) It has to do with the amount of Your Populations, how much they have skills, or needs training, work, ethics, and time management in the society that works. In All of all these things, You leaders, can make the world a better place forever one, by working together, with your society.

Chapter 2

Chapter 3

THE POWER OF
PRODUCTIVITY

I am not an economist, neither did I study these topics. But as I said, the source of all knowledge is the divine Holy God. By these times and centuries, the divine Holy God raised me to teach and preach on different topics Changing the Life of the world in all things. I want to teach about Productivity for Christians or anyone who wishes to stay productive or learn about history of Economy.

The Holy Bible says in the beginning when the divine Holy God made the first mankind's of the ground, the Holy God called them to be fruitful and multiply and fill the earth and subdue it and have dominion over the fish of the sea and over the birds of the earth.

Genesis 1:28-33). NRSV. In the beginning of all things, the divine

Holy God called the Life of the world to be fruitful and increase

in numbers. That is the blessings of the divine Holy God at the

beginning of all things. It is the divine commandment of the Holy

God to be fruitful and increase in numbers. The Holy God called the

Life of the world to make stuff out of the Life of the ground, or the

Holy Lord called them to stay creative in all things. The Holy God

called them to make all things out of the Life of the ground. Why is,

most countries is rich, and some other country poor? The answer

is, it has to do with creativity and some other things, which I will

talk about it with you in this book.

Building the Life of the world is a long journey. There are thousands

of generations passed before us, who built a better world for us.

They made all things from scratches. The Holy God gave them

the minds to think and create stuff out of nowhere. Creativity is

a Process; it takes the mind to think. The process is the thing that

makes all things work better. The Holy God called you to produce

something. Throughout history, one of the things that is important to

the world is education. Educations improve, the Life of the world.

As I said, prosperity is God's a divine calling. Do not think you

know more than the divine God. The God who formed you in your

mother's womb. When the divine Holy God made mankind's of the

ground, the Holy Lord knew all things they needed to make

their Living and the divine Holy God put everything for them in the ground. The nature of the divine Holy God is the nature of creativity. In the beginning, the divine Holy God appeared through the story of creations. The Holy Lord created all things in heavens and the earth and all things the Holy Lord created was good. The spirit of the Holy God is the spirit of creativity. Wherever there is the Spirit of the Holy God, the Spirit of the Holy God creates stuff out of nowhere. The divine Holy Lord called the Life of the world to create stuff out of nowhere.

One of the things that is good to know is that in the world we live in, Faith is the most important thing in creativity. I do not know what You know about God or the God who made the heavens and the earths, but Faith is the foundation of all things. The divine Holy God is the God who makes all things work together for good. The wisdom of the divine Holy God holds together all things and works together. The Spirit of the divine Holy God is the spirit of knowledge of all things and understanding of all things. Wherever there is the spirit of the Holy God is, there the Freedom of the Holy God is and freedom from poverty and luck of knowledge. After the fall of the first family of the ground, the divine Holy God called the Life of the world to create and make things work for them. You can be anybody in this world; what I mean is, someone who does Holy

Stuff. Faith and courage are the foundations of all things. Things work through process; what do I mean? The divine Holy God is the God of Process. There is nothing new in God, in heavens and the earths. The divine Holy God placed them before time and space; all things came to be through process. All things are the result of Process, not accident. The Holy Lord placed them before times and space and through Process they happened in the Life of the world. The divine Holy God processed them through creations and journey of the mankind. The Holy God is the One who gives You thoughts and makes them work together for good. The Holy God Process them through Your thoughts or imaginations and make them works through your creativity. Poverty is not a Gift of God; every Christian Child has to know this.

In our modern world, long ago School took over traditional ways of living. Long ago things were discovered from traditions before School or university discovered . All things were created and discovered from traditions and modernized as time went by. We all believe all things can be better through times by learning from the past. We do things better than, the past world, unless we just don't want to. The transformations of traditional ways of living to modern ways. The modern ways of Living make all things work better. But in my argument, there is something we lost from Originality, which are traditions. I do not know what you create or do in Your Life. You can be a farmer or Doctor or any other thing, but I believe there are many Universities that teaches how to create stuff and produce a society that can create stuff and makes all things works for the best. The University gives you training but they never help You create anything. You are the one who has to think and create something and make it work.

Most people do not know where money comes from. They think the government makes money. Government do not make any money or do not just print money. The one who makes money is the society; society creates money. You are the one who can make money. The modern ways of governing were transformed from traditional ways of governing. According to traditional storytellers, long ago, there was no money. The society exchange goods with each other to get what they want. That means, if You have corn, you can take some corn to the market and get something equivalent to the worth of your corn, maybe cloth or salt. Later, the government started creating money from Gold and silver and bought goods from the society and sell them back to the society. Then, that is how they started buying and selling stuff with money and the government started to control money and the markets. This process of buying and selling with money went through Process. From government to individuals started buy and sell goods. This will give you a little bit background about money or buying and selling.

From traditional ways of Living the modern ways of Living improves of a way of Living of the worlds and its economy. Long ago, productivity only depends on a way of traditions. Those days they did not have the factory that we have today. The number of Products they produced was limited. But, in our world today, productivity improved through modern ways of technology which is a Process of education and creativity—these modern ways of education and creativity improved life and transformed the Economy.

Economical transformations have to do with all things. It has to do with transforming society and Economy through educations. Transforming Economy and society through stabled and most influential governing systems in the world. It has to do with producing a society that can create and produce something in the world. Having these kinds of Society improves the Economy and a way of modern Living. One of the things to take note of is, all things involve a Process. Improving on a thing is not what you can achieve overnight; it is a Process it is a process that makes things works. For most undeveloped countries things to know is to improve all these things, taking your Society and governing systems in these directions are most important to You. Making all things works together to Improve Economy and a ways of modern Living. This means, if You build a Factory and You don't have a society that knows how to operates the machinery, it does not work. So, producing a Society with great education and well trained in all things helps Your Economy to improve. Which means, producing an educated Society, a Society that can create and make things work together, improve life and building a piece of machinery that can help the Economy and Transform. There are ways of transforming framers Life, a way of transforming a house builder's creativity. There is a ways of transforming road builders and transportations. There is a ways you can transform the Clothing industry and other industry to transform and grow Your Economy. So, transformations have to do with moving from Point A to Point B and who to transforming Economy in all ways.

For most developed Countries, the most important to know is how to transform and Produce a Society, that is educated, can create and makes all things work together to transform to the next generations without falling. How to transform all things through improvement without falling.? The easy thing in Life is falling, and sometimes most people loves, the easy pass, maybe the pass of falling. For these reason, transformations has to do with Society, you have to transform all things together. Transforming your Society and creativity all together to the next generations is the Key. That is how the Economy improves and grows. Things doesn't work with wishful thinking. It only works with reality and hard works. The divine Holy God who made You and created You with great gift, knowledge, and skills. The only thing you want is how to improve what You are already gifted at through modern educations systems, in order to make it work. Knowing what You do is the most important place to be in, creating a society that knows what they do, is the greatest thing.

In all these, one of the things we lost from traditions is faith and Courage. Nothing works without Faith and courage. Understanding these terms means understanding the wisdom of God, the God who made the heavens and the earth. The God who made You in your mother's womb. Faith keeps all things together and makes them work all together. Faith stands on knowledge, knowing what You do and makes them work without falling. Transforming all these things together is the most difficult things to the next generations without falling. Throughout history, one generation raised, the other generations failed. Maybe they did not know how to keep and maintain transformations in all things to the next generations.

The Presence of the Holy God transforms one generation to another generation. All things have to work together in order to create, improve and transform all things. You have to know what You do, you have to have knowledge or educations. You have to create, improve and make things work. You need to have the Presence of God and Faith and Courage to make all things work. Most people have their own belief systems, whether right or wrong, certain things of Faith they follow. Christians Producing Product is not only enough, but You also have to have Faith and Trust in God from the beginning of all things to the Hopes of all things. You have to Trust the Lord from Productions to sell and transforming the blessings to the next generational as a great economy. Most people work in manufacture or in your own business. You know what I am talking about. You can lie to Yourself; You have to make things work. Productivity is not only enough, if You do not sell; it is just a waste of time and energy. From the beginning, of creativity, productions , building as great Economy and transforming the world. Most people open manufactures, and they fail and Close. The center of the Life of the world is Faith and work; you have to keep these two together. Knowing what You do and building on Faith is the best thing You can do. One of the things You have to know is You can't control anything. Falling comes through many ways. Just like in our times today, the Covid19 flailed many companies around the world. You can't control the world we live in. When it comes to quality, the most important thing in life is quality, of all things and faith in work makes all things better.

In your Society, the Presence of the divine Holy God, Faith and courage is one of the most important things. One of the things You have to know is, you are naturally born of God or made by God. You are not made by humans or manufacturers . In order to make all things works together You have to know the nature of the laws of God in order to fallow them, to make all things works together. Creativity is the most important thing in Life, it's the most important things in building and transforming Economy. When it comes to productivity it has to do with the needs of the Life of the world. Something that can help and improve lives. The divine Holy God is the God who called You to Bless You. The God who called to Bless the works of Your hands. No body born rich or poor. Do not take me wrong some people have a generational money. Money is not a blessing; it can be dangers to You. Blessings is what God has giving You, what You can do by yourself. Most people create Economy from nothing or little things. They multiplied and increased it. Blessings is when You become a Blessings to other people. If You believe and hard work all things are possible, there is nothing that is not impossible in these world. If we are willing to work and make them work all things are possible. As, a leader I always believe that they have to make all things easy for their society to make and work all things. Some people just trying to make things hard for You. The divine Holy God is the God who called You to Bless You. He is the God who called You to be a Blessings to a Nations. He is the God who called You to guide You. The blessing of the divine Holy God is, throughout generations. The divine Holy God has to work throughout generations. The call of the divine Holy God the call of creativity and the call throughout generations. As, a nations the Holy God called You to be a blessing throughout generations. You have to produce a generation that create and maintain all things to the next generations and creating a society that create and produce and transform Economy has to do with the divine Holy God. The divine Holy God has to raise them. As, a Christian nations you have to continue raising with the Holy Lord. As, the Holy Lord said to Jerusalem, O Jerusalem raised up shake of your dust rise, free yourself from the Chains of your neck, daughter of Zion. 52:2). NIV, NRSV. The Holy Lord has to raise You and your generations. The Holy Lord has to raise them in all things. The Holy Lord has to raise them with great Faith and courage. The Holy Lord has to Raise them with great skills. Faith has to work in our society, for faith Produce courage and courage makes all things work. The divine words of the

Holy God and the presence of the Holy God inspires the world. The divine Holy God called You to be great and the divine Holy God called the Christian nations to be a great nations. The Holy God called them to do great things and faith makes You, do great things.

One of the things you have to know is blessings is not only materials. The Blessings of the divine Holy God is in all things. After the Holy God called the Lord's people out of the land of Egypt, the Holy Lord said them, if You obey me and fallow me whatever You touch, I will Bless For You. Deuteronomy 28:8). Deut 30:9). NRSV. The blessings of the divine Holy Lord is a divine Blessings and a divine calling. The divine Holy God called You to bless You. The blessings of the Lord's people is a call of the divine Holy Lord. The Holy Lord called them to be a bless them and their offspring. The divine Holy God called all Christian Child to produce something, and the divine Holy God called them to bless, the works of their hands. There was the story of Jesus the bible says, he was hungry in the morning when he was returned to the city, he was hungry, And seeing fig tree by the side of the road, he went it found nothing to eat on it but leaves. Then he said to it, may no fruit ever come from you again. Then the fig tree withered at once, When the disciples saw it they were amazed saying how did the fig tree withered at once. " Then Jesus said to them if you have faith and don't doubt not you do what I have done even you say to these mountain be lifted up and thrown into the sea, it will be done. Matthew 21: 18:23). NRSV.

The divine Holy God called all Christians Life with great authority. The Holy God called them to be fruitful and multiply in all things. The Holy God Called them to command things on the earth and in heavens. The Holy Lord called their Life to be fruitful and multiply. At the same times the divine Holy God is the God who Blesses and cures. The Christian Life is planted on the words of the divine Holy God. The Holy God planted them in the beginning to be fruitful and multiply. The Holy Lord made the desert blossom, the mountains straight the God of Israel is his name. The God who Appeared to Abram, Jacob and Isaac. The Holy God made the wilderness to be fruitful. The God of Israel guided them in away of Prosperity. The divine Holy God blessed whatever they touched. He made them multiply and increased in numbers. The blessings of the Holy Lord chased them out of nowhere. They were overwhelmed by the blessings of the Holy Lord and the presence of the Holy Lord. The Lord of host is with his people, the God of Americans, the God of Europeans, the God of Canadians, the God of south Americans, the God of Christina nations, the God of hosts is his name. The God of Hebrew.

The Holy Lord called you to do something great things in this world. He called you to be build a great economy. Building a great economy has to do with all things, it is a transformational thing, from point A to Point B. From going to School and getting training in order to produce something or make something works. It has to do with your imaginations to making into reality. It has to start with your thinking, transforming your thinking into productivity. Whether it's making a clothes, or making a car, or shoes or whatever its. It has to go through process, from thinking to transforming into productivity. These is how the world built, out of nowhere. The words of the divine Holy God and the Presence of the Holy God inspires You. Faith in the divine Holy God give You courage and hopes to make the imposable possible. The divine Holy God, the God who called You drive you to your destiny, making the imposable, possible. The Holy Lord said to Jeremiah what do you see Jeremiah.? And Jeremiah said I see a branch of an almond tree, then the Lord said to him you have seen very well. Jeremiah 1: 11). NRSV). The Holy Lord called You to see something and whatever the Holy Lord help you see; the Holy Lord will help you come to reality. The Holy Lord did not just call you to life. You are divine born of the eternal God, the God who called you to these Life and to the eternal Life. The divine works of the Holy God is a generational works. The divine Holy God transform all things together from generation to generations. The Holy God knows you need clothing, housing, transportations, and all things in order to live and serve the divine Holy God from generations to generations. The blessings of the Holy God is in all things, the divine Holy God blessed as in all things and the Blessings of the Holy God goes throughout generations.

The Life of the world depend on the Creativities of the human's kinds. The humankind of the ground have to make all things in order Life work for them. They have to create and produce and process it and transform into build the Life of the world and its Economy. Without creativity there is no Economy. Your Economy depend on how much your society creates, produce, and transform into building the Life of the world and its Economy. In the modern ways of buying and selling with money. If there is no productions government don't just print money. In order a government to run a country, the amount of money they print and the number of productions they can produce, maintain transform into building the Life of the world and its Economy has to balance. The amount of the Productions of their country and the amount of money they Print for buy and selling has to balance in order to balance the Economy. These modern ways of governing systems buying, and selling's want through Process and it is still not Perfect. As, I say all things have to work together in order to create and transform all things and the most important things is creativity and how to create, produce, transform into building the Life of the world and its Economy. In the modern ways of building Economy, all things have to do with school systems producing Society that can creates, maintains, produce process it and build the Life of the world and its Economy.

Creativity and Productivity is a very key to any Economic growth and Life sustainability.   Job creations and transforming the Life of the world through modern ways of quality educations. In our modern world the greatest tools in building Economy and the Life of the world is through the transformations quality educations and building of industries. The revelations of industrialization growth and transformed the Life of the world and its Economy. In our modern world, the building of industries and creativity transformed the Life of the world and its Economy. The thinking minds and creative minds of the mans and womens of the ground discovered the power of creativity in industries and they create and build great industry for the building of the Life of the world and its Economy. Building industries and the Life of the world is a Process. From thinking into creativity and productions and building the Life of the world and its Economy. The divine Holy God is, the God who inspires You and give You joy, peace and courage in order to do the things, that is impossible to do. The divine Holy God called You to do great and doing great is through Productivity and creativity. Productivity and creativity Change the Life of the world and its Economy. As, a nations You have to stay creative and Productive. You have to build the Life of your peoples and the Life of Your country through creativity and Productivity. There is no Life without creativity and Productivity. The Life of the world depends on the Creativity and Productivity of the Life of the world.

The divine Holy God called You to do great. The Holy God called You to build a great nations and building a great nations is, through creativity and Productivity. The Holy God called You to believe, in the divine Holy God, the God who made the heavens and the earth and that is all in it. Faith makes all things possible, things in heavens and the earths. The Holy divine God called You to Bless You. The divine Holy God called You to trust in him alone. For God is the God who does amazing things, through You. God is the God who made away in the wilderness. He is the God who feed thousands, in the wilderness. The divine Holy God called You to build the Life of the world and its Economy out of nowhere. The Holy God called You to build through creative means. The divine Holy God called

You to trust the Process and your hard work in creativity and Productions. The divine Holy God called You to Bless the works of Your hands and your minds and healthy. The divine Holy God called You to make You a Blessings to a nations and generations that is yet come. Do not doubt about what God can do, believe You can do great. The greatness of the world and its Economy is in You, it's not anywhere else. The greatest treasure of the Life of the world is in You, not anywhere else. The Holy Lord will bless whatever You have and multiply it and make it a blessing to a nation. You are a blessing to a nations, a blessing to Your community. You have to learn how to trust in the Lord through the Process in order the Holy Lord will bring the treasure out of You, to build the Life of the world and its Economy. My friends, if You are not Christian come to Jesus, he will bless You. He will anionite You, with knowledge and understanding of all things, things in heavens and the earth. If You want to discover some things, no one did, Just come to him, he will show you the ways and Guide You. More than anything else, he wants to save You first. He wants to save You from death, and the works of the devil.

My friends, as I say Creativity and Productivity is the key to Economy Growth and sustainability. In order Your Economy to grow, your country has to create, Produce and transform into building the

Life of the world and its Economy. With a little money, you have to create, Produce and tread in order to build the Life of the world and its Economy. Productivity and creativity growth your Economy and its sustainability. So, for all world leaders, my Prayers for You is, how to growth Productions and creativity in your country.? For the third world country, how to build, a research in stations, within the University You already have, how to transform quality educations in a global standard. How to Bring Your society into Creativity and Productions in a Global standard.? How to improve quality Productions within Your country for global tread systems.? How to transformer your society from educations into Creativity and Productions in modern ways of industrializations. As, I said it's a Process and You have to trust the Journey until You get to where You are going. There is no over night success, its all through Process, things work. For the G20 country how to restore all things to transform to the next generations.? Restoring the research intuitions, restoring, school systems to its highest quality standard. Restoring manufactures with new ideas and keep inspiring the world with new ideas, with high quality standard. How to create more and produce more with high quality standard for Global treading systems in order to build the Life of the world and its Economy. How to restore Your finical systems in with a better idea, in order to balance Your economy and life sustainability. ? According to my discover, you can restore all things, to Produce More for global tread systems in order to strengthen the Economy and grow. You can also Print More money that runes in Your Country, if the Productions is high, in order to growth Your Economy and strengthening it. But You have to balance both. The more your production is high, the more you can Print money. You can keep creating, a New discover works in order to create the New future, creating a New University, a new Company thing like that in order to create build the future and transform the Economy. More than anything, you know more than I know.)

These is what is a Power of Productions means my friends, Hope You learn something from me and God Bless You.

HOW TO TRANSFORM ECONOMY

As, I said the building of Economy is a Process. Throughout history the world was built through transformations, from traditional ways of Living into modern ways of Living. From traditional ways of marketing system to scientific modern ways of marketing systems. As, I said, long ago there is no so-called government. The people of the old age, where governed themselves according to their own traditions, life all depend on traditional ways of Living. There was no science, there was no schools, things like that. Through times a modern way of governing systems were discovered and transformed into a modern way of governing systems. From traditional ways of storytelling, or learning about religions, they discovered school and transformed into a modern way of teaching and learnings. As, I said, all things are a Process, it has to go through process. As, I said, in the divine Holy God, the God who made the heavens and the earth there is nothing is new, all things are there in the beginning of all things to the Hopes of all things. Even, the things, that is yet happen, they are not new, in the divine Holy God. They are already there in the divine Holy God, God placed them in the beginning of all things and the Hopes of all things. In the divine Holy God, all things have to go through Process and transformations and that has to do with you and the Life of the world.

In these days and ages all things have to do with schooling systems now we are at stage of, how to transform Economy and the Life of the world through the modern ways of School systems. In the old ages, they transformed the Life of the world and its Economy from traditional ways of Living in governing into modern ways of governing and school systems. The traditional ways of creativity were transformed into a modern way of creativity. From traditional ways of creativity, transformed into a modern way of creativity, through transformations of manufactures. One of the things good to know is, taking the things that you do seriously is a way of doing things right. The divine Holy God is the God who transform all things, things in heavens and the earth and the Holy Lord works through the Life of the world and the Life God's peoples. As, I said,   the source of all knowledge is the divine Holy God alone. Throughout history the divine Holy God transformed the Life of the world in all things to the Hopes of all things and the transformational works of the divine Holy God is a generational transformation through Process. The divine Holy God transform all things to generation to generation through Process. The Process, that you don't understand, but in reality, from your thoughts to creativity and productions, all things go through Process. (Hope You will understand little.)

As, I said, one of the things we lost from traditional ways of creativity and transforming economy through creativity is we lost Faith and courage. For Faith, produce courage and courage produce quality. The transformation of the divine Holy God throughout history is through the works of Faith, the people of Faith transformed all things, from traditional ways of doing stuff to a modern ways of doing stuff. As, I said, all people have a way of their own believing systems, whether its right or wrong. Faith in the divine Holy God makes You a better person.   Faith in the divine Holy God make things that You do, do it better. Faith in the divine Holy God opens your mind and hearts to all kinds of knowledges and understanding. The Holy bible says I see I Have Chosen Bezalel Son of Uri, the

Son of Hur, of the tribe of Judah. And I have filled him with the spirit of God with wisdom, understanding, with knowledge and with all kinds of Skills. Exodus 31:3). Isaiah 11:2). Daniel 1:17). NRSV. Producing a society of faith in the divine Holy God can transform all things to the next generations. It can transform Economy to the next generations, for faith in the divine Holy God produce skillful, knowledgeable and all kinds of things understanding generations. The divine Holy God works through you sometimes through creative means.

The modern kinds of transformations has to do with all kinds of transformations how to transform all things together.? As, I said, the modern ways building the Life of the world and building Economy was transformed from the traditional, ways of building the Life of the world and traditional ways of building Economy. As, I said, the divine Holy God gave you, the spirit of creativity, knowledge, wisdom and all kinds of understandings. The transformation of Economy has to do with creativity. The Process of Producing and creating a Society that can create and produce and transform the Life of the world and its Economy. Producing a Society that can create and produce something has to do with the modern ways of Schooling systems, where they can learn and modernize create and Produce and transform the Life of the world and its Economy. Producing a society of Faith, educated society that can create, produce and maintain and transform the Life of the world and its Economy to the next generations. One of the things, good to know is, Life doesn't work with wishful thinking, its only works with reality. Whatever you understand and discovered you have to make it reality through creative means. You have to make it work, you have to make it work throughout creative means.

The modern ways of creativity and productions with the manufacture improved the Life of the world and its Economy. From productions to creativity and processing and producing maintain quality, sustainability and transformed into building the Life of the world and its Economy. As, I said, in all these Faith is very important, the divine Holy God is the source of all things, things in heavens and the earth.   Building confidence is a best part of productions. Most people they do not believe in their idea or dream. There is no overnight success in creativity it's the Process that makes things work. Its is the practice that makes things work. You have to start to believe in your idea, try turn into reality. If its has to go through the modern ways of schooling systems process, learning, Practicing and make it reality. Bring it to creativity, and productions and building the Life of the world and its economy. Transformations has to start with your thinking, process it, make it reality and create and Produce and transform into Economy and building the Life of the world. All people are called to create something, but some people become creative, but some people don't. Anyways not everyone has to be creative, some people work in productions how to improve quality of productions, sustainability and transform economy through improvement of the Productions.

One of the greatest tools for Economic growth and transformation is the Global treads. Through global treads systems you can transform and growth your Economy. If productivity increase transformed into treads and Economy, then then government can increase printing money in their country. The more productivity and sells increase the more the amount of money the government can Print every year. You can argue about these with any Economist, if they have better answer for these.?). The Economy of the Life of the world was built throughout history through Process. As, I say all things are all about transformations, transforming the Economy to the greatest and sustainable Economy for all people. These is a very key to all the world, how to transform the Economy to the greatest sustainable economy.? As, leader You cannot build Economy by yourself, it has to do with the society as I said. But you can lead them with knowledge to transform the Economy to the greatest and sustainable Economy. The world needs greatest leaders who can lead them with great knowledge to the greatest future. Throughout history the world was shaped and build through the thoughts of the mans and womens of the ground. Your thoughts and imaginations have a great impact in the Life of the world and the mankind's. The Holy divine God called you to build the Life of world and the divine Holy God will give you a great knowledge to understand all things and discover all things in order to build the Life of the world and its Economy.

In our modern ways of building the life and of the world and its Economy the transformations of educations and creativity has big role in transforming the modern ways of building the Life of the world and its Economy without losing traditions of Living Faith. In these modern worlds the transformation of Economy is through educations and scientific ways of creativity and productions. Job creativity, in order to growth productivity without losing quality. Economy is transferable, from one generation to another generations. They way to transform is through creativity and improving quality educations without not losing traditions of Living the Christian Faith, prayer and courage. By being obedient to the divine Holy Lord, the God who called you to build the Life of the world and its Economy. Raising a generation with great skills and courage who can create and build the Life of the world and its Economy. In the modern ways of transforming Economy and building the Life of the world, quality educations and creativity have big roles in transforming the Economy. The divine Holy Lord is the God who called You to give You success. The Holy God is the God who called You to Bless the works of Your hands and Your health. If God want to bless You no one can stop him. As Paul said in his writing if God is for us who can be against us. Romans 8:31). NRSV). As, I said, if You believe and work hard anything is possible in these worlds. The divine Holy God transform the world and its Economy through the works of our hands. As, the Holy Lord said to his people if you obey the voice of the Lord, serving his commandment the Lord God will set You high above all the nations of the earth blessings shall come upon you and overtake You if you obey the Lord your God. Deut 28:1-3). Deut 28:4-14). NRSV.)

In these day and ages, transformations and building of the Life of the world is through quality educations, influential trading systems in all over the globe. Improving productivity without losing its quality and transformed into building the Life of the world and its Economy. Rising a generation of creativity and faith with courage growth and transform the Economy and build the Life of the world. The divine Holy God transform through the works of our hands and the divine Holy God called us to build the great economy. The American Economy was transformed and build through the revelations of

Industry and educations. Most of it has to do with the reformations of the Church medieval generations, when started to build a modern way of learning and creativity 500 years ago. From traditional ways of building Economy and the Life of the world to modern ways of building the Life of the world and its Economy. Through the call of the Lord's people, the Holy Lord build the Life of the world and its Economy. As, I said, the Holy God called them to give them knowledge and all kinds of understandings. The divine Holy God called them and gave them a Promises to guided them and be with them, to build the Life of the world and its Economy.

Through the modern ways of educations and industrial revaluations they transformed the Life of the world from traditional ways of building the Life of the world and its Economy. Creativity is all about understanding the insight of knowledge or discovering the things that no one has seen before or discovered before. One of the things, I want you to understand is that, don't be surprised by the modern technology and industry that You see in our world today. The divine Holy God called the Lord's people, to discover and built the world in all things better than we see today. The divine Holy God called You to think better and its always good to understand that, nothing is parament in these worlds, things Change from century to century, time Changes them. The old stuff goes away, and the new things goes on. The divine Holy God is the God who does new things throughout century and the divine Holy Lord does new thing through the call of God's people. Isiah 43:1:18 NRSV. But, now thus say the Lord he who crated you, O Jacob he who formed you, O Israel Do not fear for I have redeemed you, I have called You by your name, you are mine, do not remember former thing, consider the things of old. I am about to do new things, now it springs forth, do you not perceive it. The divine Holy God is the God who does new things and the divine Holy God called You to trust in the divine Holy God. Jesus said," I am the True Vine, and my father is a winegrower abide in me as I abide in You, just as the branch cannot bear fruit by itself unless it abides in the vine neither can you unless you abide in me. John 15:1;10). NRSV.). You cannot do anything without the divine Holy Lord, as a nation and as individual you cannot do anything without the Holy Lord. What does these mean.? The divine Holy God is the God who holds all things together, in God's wisdom. Building the Life of the world and its Economy is not only building industry it has to do with the divine Holy God. Unless the divine Holy God made you Prosper, sometimes even if you build industry, it is hard to prosper. As, I said, in a modern ways of productivity and creativity through industries we lost Faith and courage. You cannot change, the natural laws of the divine Holy God or the natural commandment of the divine Holy God. The natural divine commandment of the Holy God holds all things together, things in heavens and the earth. In order for you to succeeded and prospers you must obey the natural divine Commandment of the divine Holy God through your Faith or traditional, which most country practice their own traditional ways.

Building the Life of the world and its Economy depend on the Lord's people and the divine Holy God. The divine Holy Lord is the vine and the Lord's people is the branch, just as the branch cannot bear fruit unless it abides in the divine Holy Lord. . The world has to abide in the Holy divine God, in order to bear much fruit, it can be spiritual fruit, economical fruit anything, you have to abide in the divine Holy Lord. The divine Holy God is a winegrower, the divine Holy God is the God who called the Life of the world to prospers and build the Economy of the world through the works of your hands. The divine Holy God called the Life of the world to abide in the Holy divine Holy Lord and the Holy Lord will bless You in all things, to generation to generations. You have to trust in the divine Holy Lord, the Holy Lord will bless You. As, the Holy Lord said to Moses take some of the elders of the Israel and take your hand staff with which you stuck the Nile and go I will stand there before you by the rock at Horeb, strike the rock water will come out of it for the people to drink. Exodus 17:6). NRSV). You have to trust the Holy

Lord and do something in whatever is in your hands and I believe the Holy Lord will bless You. If you want to change the world, you just have to trust the Holy Lord and do something. Most people spend their time in praying but in the call of the divine Holy God You have to do all things in order for God to Bless You. You have to work hard, harder than anyone else and keep on praying while you work hard, and God will prosper the works of your hands. If You have to study, you have to study more than anyone else and keep on praying, obeying the Lord's and the Holy Lord will bless what You do.

The divine Holy God called You to build the great America, the Holy God called You to build the great Europe, South America, Canada, Jerusalem, Australia, Afrika, Asia and the Life of the world. As, I said, building the Life of the world and its economy is a Process. As, I said, building the life of the world and its Economy was transformed from traditional ways to modern ways of building the Life of the world and its Economy. The transformation of modern educations transformed the modern ways of building the Life of the world and its Economy. The transformations of industrializations transformed from traditional ways of creativity and producing into modern ways of creativity and producing through industries transformed the world and its Economy. The divine Holy God is the God who does all things, God is the God who made the heavens and the earths. The Holy God can do anything, in this world. For the divine Holy God nothing takes Process. But the greatest Challenge throughout history to the divine Holy God is, Change the minds of the Life of the world. As, I said, since the divine Holy God called the mans of the ground to a living, the Holy Lord build the Life of the world and its Economy through the mans and womens of the grounds. For the divine Holy God, in order to build the Life of the world and its Economy the Holy God has to Change the minds of the life of the world. The minds of the Life of the world has to Change in order to build and the Life of the world and its Economy. In order to transform the Economy of the world and the Life of the world, the divine Holy God has to Change the Life of the minds of the Life of the world. The divine Holy God has to Change the way you think, and the Holy Lord has to give you knowledge in order for you to build the Life of the world and its Economy. The divine Holy God has to call You to believe all things are possible, in the divine Holy God. Throughout history brining the mans and womens of the ground to these point is the greatest Challenge for the Holy God. The Holy divine Lord has to take them through Process in order to Change them and the Life of the world and its Economy. Transformation and Change is not overnight working it's a Process, sometimes one generation to another generations. Building the Life of the world and its Economy is not overnight success, sometimes from one generation to another generations. In order for the divine Holy God to Change the Life of the world and You the Holy Lord has to take you through Process and the Process is the things that Changes You and the Life of the world. These Process sometimes takes to one generation to another generations. In order for the divine Holy Lord Change the Life of the Lord's people, the Holy Lord has to call Moses and Change Moses. Through the call of Moses, the Holy Lord people get into the Promise land and build the Promises land from scratch and its Economy. This building of the Promises land was a Process from one generation to another generations. The divine Holy God Changed Moses, Out of tending the flock Jethro his Father in law, the Holy Lord appeared to him in flames of fire with burring up bush, the Holy bible says now Moses said I will go and see these strange sight, why these bush does not burn up, when the Holy Lord saw Moses was turned around to see the burning up bush, the Holy Bible says the Holy Lord Called Moses, Moses, Moses" and Moses said Here I am" Then the Lord said I am the God of Your Father, the God of Abram, the God of Isaac and Jacob. Then the Holy Bible say, then Moses was afraid to Look at the divine Holy God. Exodus 3). That where the divine Holy God Changed Moses, Moses from tending the flock of Jethro, the Holy Lord called Moses to leadership where he can lead the Lord's people to the Promise land throughout the wilderness. The divine Holy God called Moses to Faith.

Changing your imaginations is Changing the Life of the world. You have to be able to think big and do big. You have to be able to believe in God, can do more than You, think and believed. Remember the Holy Lord is able. The Holy Lord can do anything by your hands and minds. The Holy Lord can prosper the Life of the world through you. Your faith and believes Change the Life of the world in all things. Your knowledge, and creativity Changes the Life of the world and its Economy. Your Courage and hard works Change the Life of the world and its Economy. The divine Holy God Changes the Life of the world and its Economy through your imaginations, believes, Faith and hard work. If you believe and obey the Holy divine God all things are possible. The Holy bible says Jacob straggled with the divine Holy Lord. After he had sent them across the stream, he sent over all his possession. So, Jacob was left alone and a man wrestled with him till day break, But Jacob said to him " I will not let you go unless You bless me. "The man asked him what is Your name."? Jacob, he answered Jacob" then the man said to him, "Your name no longer Jacob but Israel struggled with God and with human and have overcome." Genesis 32:22). NRSV). If You struggle with the divine Holy God, the Holy Lord will bless You. Blessings is from the divine Holy Lord, and as I have said the Blessings of the Holy Lord is a generational and divine Blessings. The divine Holy God is the God who raises You in all things. The divine Holy God is the God who raised the Lord's people in all things. The divine Holy God called the Life of his people in the beginning of all things to bless them and to be with them.

Transforming Faith and quality educations to the next generations is transforming the Economy to the next generations. The next generations is the one, who build the Life of the world and its Economy. Raising generations, that can create, Produce and build the Life of the world and its Economy. Creativity, Productions, and industrializations transforms Economy and build the Life of the world. More than anything else, you have to trust in God, that the Holy God can do more than, you have done in the past. Job creativities maintain quality, build the Life of the world and transform the Economy. The transformations of Economy as I say it is a Process, from Point A to Point B. From creating the society that can think, create, Process, Produce and build the Life of the world and its Economy. From transformation through modern technology and industrializations into global Market. The building of the Life of the world has to be throughout generations, every generations has to build the Life of the world and its Economy. Ever generations have to be inspired by the divine Holy God, in order to do the impossible possible. They have to be faithful the God who called them to bless them and prosper them. The divine

Holy God works throughout generations. The divine Holy God called You to be Faithful to the divine Holy God.

Dear friends, I hope You share these books with your community in order to inspire these generations with the knowledge of the divine Holy God.

God Bless You and thank You Very Much.

UNDERESTANDING THE HISTORY OF ECONOMY

As, I said, the modern ways of governing and Economic development were transformed from the traditional ways of Living into modern ways of Living. Through times and Process, they transformed from traditional ways of governing and traditional ways of buying and selling into Modern ways of buying and selling and modern ways of governing. They transformed from traditional ways of creativity into modern ways of creativity. From traditional ways of storytelling, and religions teaching they discovered the modern ways of learning and teaching. Through times all things were transformed into the modern ways governing, creativity, school systems and modern of economical transformations, which they create money. The modern ways of governing systems created money, for buying and selling, things like that. As, I said, creativity and Productions is the greatest tools for any economical, transformations. They modern ways of creativity were transformed through the school transformations into industry. The creative minds and create industry for creativity. From agriculture food processing, clothing, housing, road constrictions things like that were transformed into the modern ways of Productivity and creativity through the modern ways of industrial productivity.

Economic development is not overnight success. Economy has to be built through times. Likewise, the Economy of America that we see today was built through times. It was a transformation from Point A to Point B through creative means. As, I said, the divine Holy God is the God who transformed the Life of the world throughout generations. One of the greatest economical transformations is the transformation from traditional ways of creativity into industrial ways creative of transformations. That is the things that Changed the Economy of the world. The more You have enough Product in your country the more you build the Economy. As, I said, in order the government to print money and distribute its has to match with the amount of Productions that country produce every years. Globalizations also played big role in Economic development through treads. Treads plays big role in economic developments. Educations and technology transformed the Economy big times.

Now you know, productivity and creativity is the greatest tools for Economic growth. Throughout times the modern ways of creativity and productivity transformed and build the Life of the world. The modern ways of transportations systems and road transformations to modern roads transformed from traditional ways of building the Life of the world and its Economy to modern ways of building the Life of the world its Economy. In a modern world building the Life of the world and its Economy has to do with producing a educated society that can, think process it, create and Produce to build the Life of the world and its Economy. All God's given natural resource, was processed used for Economic development and building of the Life of the world. As, I said, all things, where processed, created and produced used in traditional ways for the building of the Life of the world and its Economy and transformed into the modern ways of processing, producing transformed into Economy and building the Life of the world. In our world today building the Life of the world and its Economy depend on modern ways of scientific processing and building of industry. The history of Economics is the process or transformations of creativity and productions from traditional ways to modern scientific ways of creativity and productions through industrial ways. The transformations of productions from traditional ways to our modern ways of Productions, industrial ways of productions. As, I said, in our modern ways of building the Life of the world and productivity we lost Faith and courage in order to build the Life of the world and its Economy. For Faith, produce courage and courage make all things work. Faith makes the things that is impossible possible and praying by faith makes all things work.

As, I said, they transformed from traditional ways of , creativity and productions and buying and selling with goods. When from traditional ways of governing was transformed into modern ways of governing the government created money for buying and selling and they transformed a way of buying and selling through process. Which means, when government created money, it was very difficult for them to distribute money in the community. When they created money, government started to buy goods for society until they transformed into individual, and that want through process. The more you produce the more the Economy growth. In our modern world, all things has to do with technology, how to growth and transform the Economy with technology. How to transform and growth the Economy with modern educations in a global market. As, I said, after all things were transformed from traditional ways of governing into modern ways of governing the government created money for buying and selling and they bought goods from the Society and sell them back to the Society, in order to distribute money. Through times and Process individual started to sell and buy all things with money and transformed and developed throughout history. Through times and Process, the banking systems came, in America they created central bank. That was the transformation and Process of Economic development and buying and selling process.

As, I said, the Life of the world was built on creativity and Productivity, without creativity and Productivity there is no Economy. Economy is bulid on the amount of creativity and Productivity you are be able to Produce and creates. In order to grow and multiply the Economy every human being have to stay creative and productive. The more You are strong in Productions and quality the more your economy is strong. The more you create and Produce, the more the Economy growth. As, I said, government they can't just print money. Money has value with the amount of Production you can be able to create and Produce every year. The more you are strong in treading systems, the more Your Economy is strong and grows. The Life of the world and its Economy was built from scratch. The people who passed before us, they builed the Life of the world and its Economy from the

Scratch, in order Life work for them. The establishment of the modern governing systems a very important transformations, in the transformations of modern Economy. The Global treading systems, the exchange of currency, play big roles in economic transformations and development. The greatest transformations in the Economic transformations and development is, productivity and global treading systems. Creativity and Productivity strengthen, your economy and the values of your currency, in the global market. If you want to grow Your Economy and transform to the next generations, You have to keep strong in Productivity, quality educations, creativity and transforming all things together into the next stage, without losing Hopes and great Faith. If You believe and work hard, you can do anything. Things are, all about Your focus and inspirations, whatever inspire You, to do the things that You are called to do in Holiness.)

The transformations of the transportations, systems from traditional ways to the modern ways transformed the Economy of the world and build the Life of the world. Everything has to transform together to the next generations without falling. As, I said, the Promises of the divine Holy God is a Promises of a generational Blessings. You have to be able to create, Produce and transform into building the Life of the world and its Economy. As, I said, faith and Prayers, be obedient to the Holy Lord transform the Economy and built the Life of the world. Wherever God called You to do, whether You make a car and sells them, or You make prescriptions, Clothes, or you work in industry, whatever the Holy God Called You to do, You have to do it by Faith and knowledge, knowing what You do. You have to have great Faith on the divine Holy God, the God who made the heavens and the earth. Nothing works without Faith, even if You know what You do. As, nations You have to Trust the divine Holy God more than anything and do good things in the name of the Holy Lord and the divine Holy Lord will Bless Your land and your leaderships. If You run a Company, you have to give some money to Your faith Churches or organizations in the name of the Lord. In that way the divine Holy Lord will Bless You and Prosper You. As, I said, we lost these things, from traditional ways of building the Life of the world and its Economy, in the modern way of building the Economy and the Life of the world, practicing faith is Very important, if You want You can try and test. But, in reality, the divine Holy God called You to believe in God and believing in the divine Holy God, the God who called You to Life is through obeying the Lord by keeping his Holy Commandments. The divine Holy God called You to give You success in all things You do and Proper what You do. The divine Holy God called You to do great and the divine Holy God called You to build the Life of the world and its Economy. Don't be lazy, you can do great and build a great Economy., and the divine Holy God will give You success, in whatever You, do.

So, as I said, the modern way of building the Life of the world and its Economy was transformed into the modern ways of building the Life of the world and its Economy. The transformations from traditional ways governing into the modern ways of governing, systems which is government transformed the modern Economy and the Life of the world. The modern School systems and creativity transformed the Life of the world and its Economy. The revaluations of building industry, from traditional ways of creativity and Productions to modern ways build the Life of the world and its Economy. The revaluations of Productions through technology and treading systems transformed and build the Life of the world and its Economy. If You want to build a great world and a great Economy, You have to keep Producing, staying creative, improving quality education systems and producing a society that can create and Produce, Productivity to build the Life of the world and its Economy. You have to transform all things, faith, Hopes and courage to the next generations in order they will transform into the next generations. The Blessings of the divine Holy Lord and the guidance of the divine Holy Lord is always with You. You have to Trust the divine Holy Lord through the journey and the Process in order to build the Life of the world and its Economy.

Now You know, throughout history all things were transformed through Process, from traditions to modern ways of creativity and Productions. From traditional ways of buying and selling, to modern ways of buying and selling with money. From traditional ways of governing into modern ways of governing and money creativity. The discovery of the traditional ways of learning and teachings. The transformations of Industrializations and transformation of modern technology and creativity and Production to build the Economy and the Life of the world. The Life of the world and its Economy was built on the Creativity of the man kinds.

Thank You very Much and God Bless You, for understanding.

HISTORY OF THE HOLY GOD

The Holy God, the creator of the Heavens and the earths and that all in it, has God's own Holy History. Throughout History everyone wants to know, the History of the Holy God. Throughout history the Holy divine God is the God who made himself known. The Holy divine God want You tell God's Holy History to generations to generations. The Holy God is more than what we know and discovered. The works of the Holy divine God is more than what we know and seen and discovered. From outside of times and space, the divine Holy God is, the God who made known, the divine Holy God own self to the Life of the world.

Why I have to talk to you about the History of the divine Holy God.? Why.? Since from the beginning of the Life of the world and heavenly places from one of the greatest confusions is, who is God.? Most of You, you might say, we know the divine Holy God and the God who saved us.? The God who, Our ancestors have been worshiped and believed , Maybe on this books, I might share with You ,the History of the Holy God differently or a little bit deeper. From one of the call of the faithful people of the Lord in the beginning is telling the Holy History of the divine Holy God. The world has to hear and learn the History of the divine Holy Trinity, the divine Holy God who revealed himself. The heavens and the earths have to know and had knew who the divine eternal Holy God is.? Let go back to the bible, for most Christians, the Holy Bible is our foundations to tell the Holy History of the divine Holy God and story of the Holy Divine God.

The Holy bible tells us, the History of creations, starting from the mans of the ground. The first man kinds in the planet earths. After the divine Holy God made the heavens and the earths and all animals of the ground. The books of Genesis, from Chapter one to Chapter 3 is the story of Creation. The first book of Genesis is the first History of the divine Holy God. The books of Genesis tell us, about the first History of the divine Holy God. According to the books of Genesis, the History of the Holy God comes to us through creations. The Author of the books of Genesis tell us, that the divine Holy God is the God who made the heavens and the earths. It was believed that Moses was the Author of the Book of Genesis.) Moses telling the Holy History of the Holy divine God. In the history of religion, knowing history of the Holy divine God is important. If Moses is the Author of the books of Genesis, throughout the first generations of God, the people of the Holy God had been telling the story of the divine Holy God. Traditionally, people tell the story of the divine Holy God. From first family of the ground to the time of Moses at least there are about 16, 17 , generations. As, the Holy bible says, the Holy God, Appeared to His people. The Holy divine God gave his people revelations of who the divine Holy God is. The people of the Holy divine God tell the story of the divine Holy God. In the history of religion, knowing the history of the Holy God and the history of religion is important. Knowing the Coming of the divine Holy God, to the life of the world is important. According to the Holy bible, the first theologian who wrote about the Holy God is Moses. Noah wrote the story of the Holy God , through the Ark, the ark of God. Joshua 4:4:8). NRSV and said to them, "Go over before the ark of the LORD your God into the middle of the Jordan. Each of you is to take up a stone on his shoulder, according to the number of the tribes of the Israelites, to serve as a sign among you.

In the future, when your children ask you, 'What do these stones mean? 'tell them that the flow of the Jordan was cut off before the ark of the covenant of the LORD. When it crossed the Jordan, the waters of the Jordan were cut off. These stones are to be a memorial to the people of Israel forever."

One of things, you have to know, in the old ages, people tell story to generations to generations. The tell history. Those days maybe writing, and document skill is not yet discovered. Some, people say, writing was started, people writing on stone or trees. Maybe they discovered from drowning, drowning. Anyway, I don't have any evidence, how writing started, but the closest things is, they discovered from drowning, drowning. The Holy bible has a long History from all of other existence on the earths. The Holy bible tells as long History. The Holy bible tell us, the story of creations and the man kinds of the ground. Before the flood, there were a people who lived more than 7 seven eight generations, some of them lived for about 900 years and died. The history of the Holy Bible, from the time of creations to Noah's about 5000 years. After five thousand years we have the History of Noah and the divine Holy God. Noah has the story of the divine Holy God with him. From Noah generations to Abram there are many generations between Noah's, generations, and Abram at least more than eight, seven generations according to the Holy Bible. Genesis 10, 11,) .

After Noah's, the Holy bible tell as the History of the Holy God

with Abram.

Throughout History, from one of the greatest confusions is About

the divine God. Whether the Holy God exists. Or who is God.?

What are the human beings.? All theological questions of the exists

of man kinds and all creations. Throughout history not everyone

knew the divine Holy God, the God who made the heavens and

the earths. But, the Truth of the matter is, the divine Holy God

existed without times and space. Before the man kinds where, the

Holy God is. Throughout history, one of the greatest witness to the

existence of the divine Holy God is the works of the divine Holy

God. Throughout history the Holy divine God did not appeared to

Everyone. Not everyone understood   and discovered the revelations

of the Holy God. Throughout history, after many generations, the

History of the Holy God is only with few peoples. The Story of the

fist family of the ground, the story of Noah's and Abram. These are

the people who had encounter with the divine Holy God. The people

who told the History of the divine Holy God. The world doesn't

have to have doubt whether the divine Holy God is the God who

made the first mans of the ground. One of the things, the world has

to understand, is that.? The Holy divine God is the God who does all things. The Holy divine God does whatever pleased the divine Holy God. For the divine Holy God, there is no end or beginning. The Holy God existed without even time and space and the divine Holy God is a divine eternal Living Holy God. In history, creating the man kinds pleased the divine Holy God. The Holy bible says, after the Holy Lord made the heavens and the earths that is all it. It pleased the divine Holy God to made the first mans of the ground. The divine Holy God made History with the mans of the ground. The divine Holy God creating the mans of the ground and the all creations is the history of the divine Holy God. The divine Holy God revealing God own self is the history of the divine Holy God. The divine Holy God mixed his divine Nature with the mans of the Ground is the History of the divine Holy God.   Genesis 26:24 Genesis 15:,). Exodus 3:6). NRSV. The Holy God mixed his divine nature with dust of the ground. In the beginning of all things , the divine Holy God Speaking is the story of the Holy God and the story of the Life of the world. In the beginning of all things the garden of Eden was the story of the Holy God. In the beginning of all things, the works of the miracle of the divine Holy God the history of the divine Holy God. The divine Holy God is the God who make history and the Holy God is known by making history throughout history. The divine Holy angel of the Holy God is the history of the Holy God. The divine Holy God creating the heavens and the earths is the History of the Holy God. In the beginning the divine Holy God speaking with his people, is the History of the divine Holy God. In the beginning the call of the Life of the world is the History of the Holy God.

One of the things I want You to understand is that, before even the world and the mans of the ground existed the divine Holy God exist internal heavenly places and earth. The divine Holy God lives forever, in the divine Holy God, there is no dying and Living. The divine Holy God just exist alone, with his Holy angels in heavenly places and these divine Holy God is known for divinely Speaking, the Word which the Greek Bible says According to the Gospel of John , in the beginning there was a Word, and the Word was with God and the Word was God. NRSV. That is the Divine Holy God speaking in the beginning. The word term Logos.) Many people wonder how the Holy God created the heavens and the earths and the mans of the grounds. One of the things You have to know, is the divine Holy God is greater than and bigger than anything that You see in the world and heavenly places. The divine Holy God holds all things together in His Holy wisdom. When the divine Holy God moves things, they move. One time in history the divine Holy God called all things, together to existence . One time in the history of the divine Holy God caused the creations of the mans of the grounds.

The Holy bible tells as the divine Holy God made all things through Speaking, in another languages one time in the history of the divine Holy God, the holy God caused them to Happen. The divine Holy God made all things likes these and throughout history all theologians and the mans of Faith trying to justify the works of the divine Holy God.

One of the things, that You have to know is, throughout history the Holy divine God speaks. Throughout history the works of the divine Holy God is the witness to the works of the divine Holy God. The divine Holy God caused all things to Happen. In the early ages the names of the divine Holy God was known, El Shaddai which means the divine Holy God is can do all things. When the Holy bible tells the divine Holy God revealed himself, its not fictions. Throughout history the divine Holy God is known by revealing God own self to the Life of the world. As, I said, the divine Holy God revealed who is through creations. 2) The divine Holy God revealed who is through making the man kinds of the ground. 3) The divine Holy God revealed who is through Speaking with the mans of the ground. 4) The divine Holy God revealed who is through the Commandments and the divine Holy Laws of the divine Holy God. 5) The divine Holy God revealed who, the divine Holy God is through his Holy angels and Holy dreams and Holy Visions. 6) The divine Holy God revealed who is, through the works of the Holy Spirit by the Holy Prophets. At the ends the Holy God revealed who is, through the Promises of the call of God own son, the one who is born of Verigin Mary through the works of the Holy Spirit.

The divine History of the Holy God, the God who created the heavens and the earths is a Holy History. My dear friends and the Churches its good to write the History of the divine Holy God in Holiness. Throughout history people wrote their Story and put it in high places. The Holy Church supposed to write the History of the Holy God and put it in high places for generations, to generations. The Holy bible is the history of the Holy God and the story of the Lord's people. Throughout history generations learned the History of the Holy God and the story of the Lords people from the Holy bible. Many people come to faith, through the Holy bible. That is why it's very important writing the history of the divine Holy God, the God who appears, The divine Holy God, who created the heavens, and the earths is a divine Holy and Holiness is who the divine Holy God is.

The Holy divine God, speaking with the Lord's people is the history of the Holy God and the history of God's people. The divine Holy God speaking with Noah, is the history of the Holy God and story of the Lord's people. The divine Holy God speaking, with Abram is the history of the Holy God and the story of the Lord's people. The divine Covenant of the Holy God and the Promises of the Holy Lord with Abram and Noah is the history of the Holy God and the story of the Lord's people. The divine angel of the Holy Lord appearing to Abram and Sahara is the History of the Holy God and the History of the Lord's people. After the fall of the first family of the grounds, the Holy God appearing and giving them a Promises of saving the Life of the world from the works of the devil and recreating other humans' kinds of the ground, who will born of the divine Holy God by Faith again is the history of the Holy God and the history of the Life of the ground. The journey of the Holy Lord people with the divine Holy God is the history of the Holy God and the story of the Lord's people.

As, I said, throughout history the divine Holy God appears and make God's divine works known. The divine Holy God made known the works of heavenly places into the Life of the world. Throughout the history of the divine Holy God passed on to generations to generations. The saving divine works of the Holy God and restoring works of the Holy God passed on to generations to generations. After the divine Holy God created the heavens and the earths and the Life of the world fallen into the darkness of the world the only hopes of the Life of the world is the divine Holy God. Just like today the Life of the world is fallen into darkness and the only Hopes for these world is, the Holy divine God alone. Throughout history the history of the divine Holy God is, with his people. The revelations of the Holy God and the Truth of the Life of the world and heavenly places is, with the Lord's people. The divine Promises and Covenant of the Holy God is with his people. The divine Miracle of the Holy God is the History of the Holy Lord. The reconciliations of the Life of the world, through God's own Son Jesus the Christ is the History of the divine Holy God and the story of the Lord's people.

Lets, talk about the Holy History of the divine Holy God the God who made the heavens and the earths and the God of Jesus Christ. For the Life of the world knowing the history of the divine Holy God and understanding the Holy divine, History of the Holy God is important. Throughout history there are many god's people believed in it, and worshiped and trusted on it. There is only one divine Holy God, the God who made the heavens and the earths and the man kinds of the grounds. There is one Holy Spirit, the Holy Spirit the Spirit the divine Holy God the God who made the heavens and the earths. Throughout history there is only one, divine Holy God who appeared, the God who made the heavens and the earths and the mans of the ground. Throughout history the Life of the world divide, about who is God.? And throughout history people according to their belonging and Community they started to find Hopes and meaning on believing on something. As, I said, some people started to believe on traditional spiritual leaders in their community. They are a people who claimed to be they know everything, and they worship some kinds of Spiritual worships. Their community started to fallow such people and do whatever they told them to do. That is their Faith and believes. There are people who believed the God who made mountains and water and they started to Worship in the lakes. There are other people who made their gods from gold and statues and worshiped. There are other people who just believed in the God of Abram and Isaac.

One of the things the world did not knew is knowing history of the world and the religions believes, is important in order to understand the divine Holy God. Understanding the Story of the Holy bible and the story of the Lords people is important. Before there is a Christian Faith, Islam Faith. Their is one religion, the Faith or religion of Abram, the divine Holy God who Appeared to Abram and Jacob. The divine Holy God Appeared to Abram and Abram started to understand the divine Holy God the God who does all things. The divine Holy God made known himself to Abram and Abram find Faith on the Holy God. The divine Holy God said to Abram I am

God almighty. Genesis 17:1) The divine Holy God called him to be Blameless. The divine Holy God appeared to Noah; the Holy bible says Noah build the Ark to the divine Holy God who Appeared to him. The saving works of the divine Holy God revealed through the Ark of Noah. The Ark of Noah Saved him and His family from the Flood. As I say the divine Holy God is a divine Holy God and eternal God. The divine Holy God appears throughout history and make known his divine Holy works.

When civilizations started and people started to bulid City according to their belongings. Faith become a part of their Social and Political governing. Faith become a Part of their civilizations. They started to bulid their city based on their understanding of their Faith. Teaching and revelations always come from their spiritual leader based on their understanding of their Faith. As, I said, After Noah, the divine Holy God Appeared to Abram and Jacob. But, Abram and Jacob that time did not bulid their own City. They moved from places to places. Abram and Lot fought on Land and the Lord Separated Abram from Lot. The City of Sodom and Gomora was burned up by fire. Genesis 19:19). The divine Holy Lord Separated Abram from Lot.

Abram had two sons Isaac and Ishmael. Isaac was the Promise Child and Ishmael born becouse of the mistakes of Sahara and Abram.

After Isaac grew Up he started to dig wells. The Holy Bible says the Holy Lord Appeared to Isaac again. When Isaac dig a wells and find water the Philistines fight against Isaac. Genesis 26). The Holy divine God Appeared Abram, Isaac and Jacob and the Holy God was with them. They find Hopes and Faith on the divine Holy God, the God who Appeared to them. The divine Holy God, the God off heavenly places and eternal divine God. The divine Holy God the God off angels, the God who is almighty was with Abram, Isaac, and Jacob. The divine Holy God who made the heavens the earths and the mans of the ground appeared to Abram, Isaac, and Jacob. The divine Holy God almighty appeared to his people. That, time of Century not everyone knew the divine Holy God, the God of Abram, Isaac, and Jacob. As, I said, the other people according to their descendants and belongings they started to find Hopes and meaning in different gods.

Jacob and his family remained in the land of Egypt for about 400 years. After 400 years the Holy bible says the Holy Lord remembered God's Promises and Covent with Abram, Isaac and Jacob. When the Lord's people suffured in the land of Egypt the Holy Lord saw the Suffering of His people. The divine Holy God , the God who Appeared to Abram, Isaac and Jacob again appeared to Moses. While Moses was in the wilderness the Holy Lord

Appeared Moses and Spoke with him. When the LORD saw that he had gone over to look, God called to him from within the bush, "Moses! Moses!" And Moses said, "Here I am." "Do not come any closer," God said. "Take off your sandals, for the place where you are standing is holy ground." Then he said, "I am the God of your father, the God of Abraham, the God of Isaac and the God of Jacob." At this, Moses hid his face, because he was afraid to look at God. Exodus 3:1-5). NRSV0. Then Moses said to the Holy God, "Suppose I go to the Israelites and say to them, 'The God of your fathers has sent me to you,' and they ask me, 'What is his name?' Then what shall I tell them?" God said to Moses, "I AM WHO I AM. This is what you are to say to the Israelites: 'I AM has sent me to you.'" God also said to Moses, "Say to the Israelites, 'The LORD, the God of your fathers--the God of Abraham, the God of Isaac and the God of Jacob--has sent me to you.' "This is my name forever, the name you shall call me from generation to generation. 14). The divine Holy God revealed who the divine Holy God is, that is the names of the divine Holy God, the God who created the heavens and the earths and that is all in it. The divine Holy God revealed to Moses his divine works and divine calling of His people. As, I said, the divine Holy God, is the God who speaks and speaking of the divine Holy God is the story of the Holy God and the works of the Holy God. In the beginning of all things, the divine Holy

God is the God who speaks. He is the divine Holy God appears and speaks and the Appearing of the divine Holy God is the History of the Holy God and the history of the Lord's people. In the beginning of all things, the History of the Holy God entered the Life of the world. The divine Holy God wrote his history through the creations of the Life of the world and the mans of the ground. The calling of the Life of the Lord's people is the history of the divine Holy God and the history of the Lords people.

Throughout history the Holy divine God wants to write his divine History into the Life of the world. The divine Holy God wrote his divine History through the creations of the Life of the world. The divine Holy God wrote his history through the call of the Lord's people. The divine Holy God history is a generational history. After the fall of the call of the Life of the world, the Holy God revealed the history of the divine works of the Holy God through saving the mans of the ground from the works of the serpent and man kinds from their own self. The divine Holy God wrote the story of the divine Holy God in the heart of the Lord's people and the heart of the Life of the ground. In the beginning of all things, the divine Holy God, brought the divine History of the Holy God which is in heavens to the Life of the world. The saving of the Life of the Lords people from the lands of Egyptians is the divine saving, transforming of the works of the Holy God and the divine History of the divine Holy God.

In the beginning of all things the Holy Lord calling the Life of the world is the history of the Holy God and the history of the Lord people. The divine Holy God is with us is the story of the Holy God and the history of the Lord's people.

One of the things I want the world to understand is that understanding history of the Holy God and the history of the Lord people is important. For in the beginning of all things, the history of the Holy Lord come to the Life of the world. The divine Holy God brought the history of the Holy God from divine eternity into the world. The story of the Holy Lord come to the Life of the Lord's people. The divine Holy Lord appeared and Spoke to his people. The Holy Lord appearing to Noah, Abram, Jacob and Isaac was the history of the Holy Lord and the History of the Lord's people. The Holy Lord saving the Life of the world through the Ark of Noah was the story of the Holy God and the story of the Lord's people. The Holy Lord made history through the works the ark of saving the family of Noah's from the flood. The divine Holy Lord entering into a Covenant with Noah's and Abram is the history of the Holy God and the history of the Lord's people. The divine Holy

God calling Abram, Isaac and Jacob was the story of the holy God and the story of the Lord's people. Genesis 9;) Genesis 12;) Genesis 17:). NRSV.) The Holy Lord speaking to his people in the beginning was the Holy history of the Holy God and the Holy history of the Lord's people. The Life of the world falling into the darkness of the world and the works of Evil and the divine Holy God saving the Life of the world from the works of the darkness of the world and the devil is the history of the Holy God and the history of the Lord's people. The divine saving and transforming the Life of the world from the internal works of the devil is the story of the Holy God and the story of the Lord's people. The Holy bible says after the Holy Lord made the heavens and the earth, the Holy Lord appeared and spoke to the family of the ground. The Holy Lord gave them his divine Holy words and promises to remain in the garden of Eden. In the beginning of all things the divine Holy God calling the Life of the world to Life is the history of the Holy God and the history of the Lord's people. The divine Holy God creating the heavens and the earths and that is all in it is the history of the Holy Lord and the history of the Life of the world. One of the things is good to understand is that history is very important. The Holy Lord wanted his people to write his history. As, the divine Holy Lord said to Prophet Jeremiah thus say the Lord the God of Israel write all the words I have spoken with You. 30:1). The divine Holy Lord wanted the Lord's people to write the divine words of the Holy God. The divine history of the Holy God has to be told to generations to generations to generations. The saving works of the divine Holy God and the transforming works of the Holy God has to be told to generations to generations. The divine Promises of the Holy God that the Holy Lord is with us is the story of the Holy God and the story of the Lord people. In the beginning the Holy God with us is the story of the Holy God and the story of the Lord's people. The Promises and Covenant of the Holy Lord was always with his people. After the Holy Lord's people remained in the land of Egypt for more than 400 years and the Lord's people started to suffer and cry out to the Lord the Holy Lord remembering his Promises and Covenant with Abram and Jacob was the story of the Holy God and the story of God's people. The bible says the Holy Lord saw the suffering of his people in the land of Egypt. When the Holy Lord saw the suffering of his people the Holy Lord did not keep quiet about his people. The divine Holy Lord remembered his divine Holy Promises and Covenant with his people. The Holy Lord saw the suffering of his people and the divine Holy Lord come down again to save the Life of his people. The divine Holy God come down to save and transform the Life of the Lords people. The saving miracle of the works of the Holy God was the story of the Holy God and the story of the Lord's people. The divine Holy God come down to save the Life of his people.

He come down to transform them from the states of suffering to the states of hopes and future. The Holy Lord appearing to Moses while Moses was in the wilderness is, the story of the Holy God and the story of the Lord's people. The places of the burning up bush in the wilderness is the places of the history of the Holy God and the history of Moses. The places where the Holy Lord called Moses to Faith, to believe in the Holy God. The places, where the Holy God Spoke with Moses face to face.   The places of a Changing moment, the places where the divine Holy Lord Changed Moses. The places of the Miracle of the Holy Lord and the places where the Holy Lord revealed the Holy Lord own self.

From the beginning of all things one of the Promises of the Holy God is that after the Holy Lord made the mans of the ground the Holy God Promised the Life of the world to be with them. The Holy divine God with us and the Holy divine God with us is the history of the Holy God and the history of the Lord people. The divine Holy God is the God who makes history. The History of the Holy God is the miracle   of the Holy God. The Holy Lord divided the red sea and leading his people to the Promise land is the   History of the Holy God and the history of the Lord people. The divine Holy God feeding man from heavens his people is the history of the Holy God and the history of the Lord people. The Holy God speaking Hopes and about the future is the history of the Holy God and the of the Lord's people. As, I said, throughout history the divine Holy God is the God who made history in the Life of the world and in the Life of the Lord's people. The divine Holy God is the God who makes history in Your Life. The Holy Lord made history in the Life of the Lord's people. The Holy Divine God made history in the Life of Abram, Isaac and Jacob. The Holy Lord called Abram out of his relatives to the land the Holy Lord had called him. The divine Holy Lord called the Life of his people to history, the history of the divine Holy God. The Holy Lord called the Life of his people to his Holy Presence, to the Presence of the Holy Lord. The Holy Lord called them to the creations the Holy Lord had created, to keep it and take care of it. In the beginning of all things the divine Holy God called the Life of the world and the Life of his people to know the history of the Holy God and to the divine Holy God, the God who made the heavens and the earths. As, I said, the divine Holy God is the God who made history. The call of the Life of the world and the mans of the ground is the History of the Holy God and the history of the Lord's people. The call of the Christian nations and the Christian Churches is the history of the Holy God and the History of the Lord's people. The call of Australia, the call of Canada, Europe, south America, Africa, and middle east is the call of the History of the Holy God and the history of the Life of the world. In the

beginning the divine Gods history is with us. After the fall of the
Life of the world, the saving and transforming works of the Holy
God is the history of the Holy God and the history of the Lord's
people. In the beginning of all things the divine Holy God called
the Life of the world to know the history of the Holy God and the
presence of the Holy God. The creations of the Life of the world is
the history of the Holy God and the history of the Life of the world.
The divine Holy Lord revealing the divine Holy Lord own self to the
Life of the world and to his people is the history of the Holy God
and the History of the Lord people. The call of the Prophets of the
Holy Lord and the Prophets of the Holy Lord speaking to the Life
of the world is the history of the Holy God and the history of the
Life of the world. The Promise and the Covenant I will Bless You
and I will be with You wherever You go of the Holy Lord to the Life
of the world is, the History of the Holy Lord and the history of the
Life of the world. The Holy Lord Promised the Life of his people
to Bless them and the Holy Lord called them to be a Blessings to a
nations. When the Holy Lord called the Life of the world the holy
Lord called the Life of the world to greatness. The Holy Lord called
the Life of his people to be great. Throughout history the revelations
of the Holy God changed the Life of the world in all things. One time
coming down of the Holy Lord to the Life of the world Changed the
Life of the world and the Life of the Lord's people. The

Holy Lord revealing the Holy Lord own self to Moses and Changed the history of the Life of the Lord's people. Through the divine Holy God revealing the divine Holy God own self to Moses, the Holy Lord called his people from the places of suffering. The Holy Lord called them to the new world to the Promises land. The Holy Lord revealing the Holy Lord owns self to Moses Changed the Life of the Lord's people. The Holy Lord led them to the Promise land. The Holy Lord speaking through the mouth of God's Holy Prophets Changed the Life of his people. The Holy Lord revealing the Holy Lord own self through the angels of the Holy God Changed the Life of the Lord's people. The Holy Lord coming down from heavens through the Life of Jesus Christ Changed the Life of the Lord's people and the Life of the Christian Nations.

As, I said, the history of the Holy God is the divine Holy God is with us. Since the Holy Lord made the heavens and the earths, the Promises and Covenant of the Holy Lord is with his people and the Life of the world. Throughout history, the history of the Holy God is, the Holy Lord is with us. The Holy Lord kept his Promises and Covenant with the Life of the world. The divine Holy Lord Promised that the Messiah would be born of Verigin Mary the one who reconciled the heavens and the earth with the divine Holy God is with us, is the history of the Holy God and the history of the Lord's people. The divine Holy God fulfilled whatever he had Promised to his people and the Life of the world. Gods divine Promises making all man kinds of the Children's of the Holy God the once who did not knew the Curses of death but born of the Holy God on the mountain of Golgotha.   Therefore, brothers and sisters, since the Holy God created the heavens and the earths the Holy God is with the Life of the world. The Holy Lord is with us. The Holy Lord is with his people. The Holy Lord guided his people. When they want through the fire and the deep water the Holy Lord was with them. When they want through suffering the Holy Lord was with them. When they fought from left to right the Promises and Covenant of the Holy Lord was them. When they turned away from the Promises and Covenant of the Holy Lord, they Holy Lord Punished them and returned them to his Promises and Covenant. When they were afflicted by the Evil spirit the Holy Lord heled them and transformed them by his Holy miracle. The hands of the Holy God and the Presences of the Holy God transformed them. The divine Holy God by God own self   is, God is the God who keeps history, and the history of the Holy God is who God is. As, I said, the divine Holy Lord is the Lord who revealed God own self to the Life of the world. The divine Holy God the God who made the heavens and the earth made known the divine Holy God own self to the Life of the world. The divine Holy God made known his Holy divine Holy Law and Commandment to the Life of the world. The divine Holy Lord made known his divine Holy Covenant and Promises to the Life of the world. As, the Holy bible says throughout history the Holy divine God made known God own self to the Life of his people from times to times. From times to times the Holy Lord made known his Holy kingdom to the Life of the world. The Holy Lord called Paul, on the ways of Damascus. The divine Holy God made known himself and his Holy kingdom to Paul. The Holy Lord made known the Holy Lord own self to His Holy disciples. Act 9). Matthew 17.) NRSV. The Holy Lord raised the dead from the dead. The saving and transforming work of God revealed through the call of the disciples. The Holy Divine Lord raised the dead from the dead. The Holy Lord healed their sick's. The Holy Lord spoke on the mountains. The Holy Lord guided his people to the Promise land. The hands of the Holy God and the Presence of the Holy God divided the walls of Jericho. The Holy Lord called his people to his Holy mountains. The Holy Lord Holyfield the Life of the world and his people through the suffering of the Holy Christ. The Holy Lord called the Life of his people to greatness. The Holy Lord called them to be faithful to the Call of the Holy Lord and the Promises of the Holy Lord. For the strengthen of the Christian Life and the Church is the Presence of the Holy God and the gaudiness of the Holy Lord. The divine Holy Lord called the Life of the world to be Holy through the Holy Christ.

Throughout history the presence of the Holy God and the gaudiness of the Holy Lord was with his people.

As, I said, throughout history the Holy Lord made known the Holy Lord own self to his people to guide them, to give them a blessings and to save them from the darkness of the world and the works of the devil. The security of Jerusalem, and the Hopes of Jerusalem was the Hopes of the Holy Lord alone. The only one who saved the Life of his people and saved them from the darkness of the world and the Evil spirit was the Holy Lord alone. Dear friends the history of the Holy God is with us. The history of the Holy Lord is with the Christian nations and the world. The saving works of the Holy God and transforming works of the Holy Lord through the works of the Holy Spirit is with us. The Holy God called You to know him personally, the Holy Lord called You to know him in your Church. For knowing the Holy Lord is knowing the history of the Holy Lord and the history of the God's people. The divine works of the Holy God transformed throughout generations. God's Holy works through the life of Jesus Christ by the power of the Holy spirit transformed and renewed the Life of the world as a new creation. The Holy Lord made all things New through the suffering of the Holy Trinity. The divine work of the Holy God the God who made the heavens and the earth renewed the Life of the world as a new creations every day.

The divine works of the Holy God was fulfilled through the dying and raising of the Holy Christ. The dying and raising of the Holy Christ is the History of the Holy God and the history of the Christian nations. For knowing the Holy Christ is knowing the History of the Holy God and the history of the Holy Christ. For knowing the history of the Holy God is knowing the divine Holy God. The call of the Holy divine God is a Call of Everlasting Call and it's a call from generations to generations. The call of the Presence, the Promises and Covenant of the Holy God throughout history is with the Lord's people and the Life of the world. The divine Promises and covenant of the Holy Lord is with us. As, I said, throughout history the holy God come down to the Life of the world from times to times. The Holy God come down in many ways. 1, Sometimes the divine Holy Lord come down through the Presence of the Holy Spirit.2) Sometimes the Holy Lord come down and spoke through his Holy angels, dreams and Visions. 3) Sometimes the Holy Lord spoke through the mouth of his Holy Prophets. 4) At the end the Holy come down and spoke with his people through the Life of Jesus Christ. From times to times, the Presence of the Holy God come down to the Life of the world through the Presence of his Holy people.

As, I said, throughout history the divine Holy God Speaks, from times to times. The divine Holy Lord speaks to renew, restore and give hope to the Life of the world. The Holy Lord speaks to strengthen where there is weakness to guide and to bless the Holy God speaks. As, I said, knowing the knowledge of the Holy God and knowing the divine Holy God is knowing the history of the Holy God and the history of the Lord people. In the beginning of all things the call of the Life of the Lord's people is the call into the presence of the Holy Lord in world. Wherever there is a Christian child and the Christian Church is there is the Presence of the Holy Lord is. Wherever there is the Christian child and the Christian Churches the divine Holy Lord come down and speaks. The Holy God come down to heal, to restore, the to save Life.

Therefore, brothers and sisters as I said, the History of the Holy God is the Holy Lord is with us. The history of the Holy God is the divine Holy God made the heavens and the earth together in his Holy wisdom. The divine Holy God, the God of Jesus Christ holds the heavens and the earth together in his Holy wisdom. In the beginning of all things the divine Holy God who made known himself to the Life of his people and the Holy Lord is with us. The Holy God is the God of heavens and the earth , the Holy Lord is God on the heavens, on air, under deep water, in fire , on the earth and in hell, God is God alone. The God who can save You and guide you through all the storm of Life. The Christian Life is the kings of all things, the are the kings of deaths, the kings of the devil, the kings

of the air, the heavens and the earth. There was the story of Jesus

with his disciples going from one city to another city on the boat.

The Holy Bible says one day Jesus said to his disciples " Let us go

over to the other side of the lake' So they got into a boat and set out.

As they sailed, he fell asleep. A squall came down on the lake, so

that the boat was being swamped, and they were in great danger. The

disciples went and woke him saying Master, Master we're to drown

and Jesus get up and rebuked the winds and the raging waters the

storm subsided, and all was calm Jesus said to them, where is Your

faith. The disciples where in fear and amazement they asked one

another who is this .?" he commands even the winds and the water,

and they obey him Luke 8:20:26). NRSV. The divine Holy works

of the Holy God was fulfilled in the Life of Jesus Christ and all

Christian Child, and the works of the Holy God in the Life of Jesus

Christ is the history of the Holy God and the history of the Lord

people. The divine Holy God called the Life of the world to have

Faith on the divine Holy God the God who made the heavens and

the earth through the Life of Jesus Christ. The divine Holy Faith that

revealed through the Life of Jesus Christ makes You live.

The Holy Lord called the Life of his people to tell the story of the

Holy God. The Holy Lord appeared to his people so that they can tell the history of the Holy God. As, I said, the Holy Lord appeared

to Abram and Abram told history of the Holy God. The Holy Lord

Appeared to Jacob and Moses and they told the history of the Holy

God. When the holy divine Lord Appeared to them, the divine Holy

Lord started to Change them and the people of the Holy Lord started

to tell the works of the Holy God, saving works, the guiding works

and the Blessings works of the Holy God to the world. They started

to tell the story of the God who Appeared to them. The God who

saved them from the hand of the darkness of the world and the hand

of the devil. When the divine Holy God Appeared to them, the divine

Holy Lord called them to believe in God. The Holy God called them

to believe the unbelievable, to trust an trustable and the Holy God

was with them. Through the call of Moses, the Holy God called the

Life of his people out of the darkness of the world. The Holy Lord

called them from the places of suffering doubting to a places where

they can believe and trust the Holy Lord again. The Holy Lord called

them to have Faith again. The Holy Lord called them to believe

in God. Moses told the works of the Holy God and the wonders,

Miracle of the divine Holy Lord to the Life of the Lord's people

and the world. Through the story telling of the works of the Holy

God the Lord people and the Life of the world come to Faith again.

The Holy Lord Appeared to Paul and Changed Paul. Through the call

of the Holy Lord, Paul started to tell, teach and preach the works of the Holy God in the Life of Jesus Christ, to the Life of the world. Paul thought the   history of the Holy God. The Holy God called them to tell the history of the Holy God and the works of the Holy God to the Life of the world. After the Holy Lord called his disciples, the Holy Lord tell them to go and tell the works of the Holy God through the Life of Jesus Christ. Jesus said to them, all authority in heaven and earth has been given to me go therefore make disciples   of all nations baptizing them in the name of the Father, and the Son and the Holy Spirit and teach them everything I have commanded You. Matthew 28:16:20). NRSV).

The Faithfulness of the Holy Lord and the leading of the Holy Lord is the history of the Holy God and the history of the Lord's people. The Holy Lord called You out of dust of the ground to worship him alone on his Holy Mountain. The Holy Lord Called the Life of the world to speak of the greatness of the Holy God on his Holy Mountain. The God who Called You, is a Faithful God with the Life of the world and the Life of his people. The Holy Lord Called the Life of the world to be Faithful to the Holy Lord and the Call of the Holy Lord. In the beginning when the divine Holy Lord called the Life of the world, the Holy Lord called them to abide into the Holy Lord and to tell the history of the Holy Lord to generations to generations. The Holy Lord called them to tell the history of the Holy God and the works of the Holy God to generations to generations. The Holy God called them to speak of the Faithfulness of the Holy God, the Holiness of the Holy God and saving and transforming works of the Holy God. The divine Holy God works in as and through the Life of the mankind's in the Life of the world and heavenly places. The spirit of the divine Holy God and the presence of the divine Holy God works in the Life of the mans of the grounds and the spirit of the Holy God makes the mans of the ground a Living being in his Holy Presence. The spirit of the divine Holy God and the Presence of the Holy God renew and transform the Life of the world to the Places where the Holy God has Called them. The Promises, divine Covenant and the Faithfulness of the Holy God is the history of the Holy God and the history of the Lord's people. Throughout history the Life of the world and the Life of the Lord's people were overtaken by the darkness of the world and afflicted by the spirit of Evil. Sometimes they were overtaken by the force of the darkness of the world and turn away from the divine Holy God the God who called them. But, as I said, throughout history the divine Holy God was a faithful God to his people. The Holy God come down and saved them and transformed them from the darkness of the world and Evil afflictions to his Holy Presence. The Holy Lord send his Holy angels and raised a Prophets who can call the Lord's people out of the darkness of the world to the Presence of the Holy God. God own self come to the Life of the world through the works of the Holy Spirit in the Life of Jesus Christ and called God's people out of the darkness of the world to his Holy Mountains. The Holy Lord called Moses and called God's people out of the darkness of the world to the Promises land and worshiping the Holy Lord in his presence again. The Holy God called them and forgave the sins of the Life of the world by the blood of the lam, the blood of Jesus Christ. The Holy Lord Holyfied the Life of his people and the Life of the world by the blood of Jesus Christ. The divine Holy God freed the Life of the world and the Life of the Lord's people from the darkness of the world and the Captivate of the power of sins and the curses of sins by the blood of Jesus Christ. The Holy Lord redeemed the Life of the world and the Life of God's people through the suffering of the dying and raising of the Holy Christ, the promises Child. As I said, the history of the Holy God is the Faithfulness of the Holy God and the Faithfulness of the Lord's people. The works of the Holy God works throughout generations to the promises of the Holy God to generations to generations.

Dear Brothers and sisters, what can I say more than this to You. The history of the Holy God is the divine Holy God is with us throughout generations. The faithfulness, Covenant and Promises of the divine

Holy Lord is with the Life of the world throughout generations. The Holy Lord kept his divine Faithfulness, Promises and Covenant with the Life of the world and the Life of his people. The Holy Lord was faithful to them, when they turn away from the Lord and did evil did the Holy Lord punished them and called them back to his promises and Covenant again. The Holy Lord called them back to keeping his Holy Promises and Covenant in holiness again. The Holy Lord came down to save You. The Holy Lord did miracle to save You. The Holy Lord send his Holy angels, his Holy Prophets who can preach to you the saving works of the Holy God and transforming works of the Holy God. The Holy Lord send his Holy son Jesus the Christ in order to save You and Transform the Life of the world to the presence of the Holy God and Promises of the Holy Lord. The Holy Lord divided the red sea in order the people of the Lord get to the Promise land. The Holy Lord made history in order to save the Life of the world and Your Life. The Holy Lord was crucified and dead and raised in order to save You and the world. The Holy Lord appeared to Abram, Moses and Jacob and made history. The Holy Lord destroyed the walls of Jericho and rebuild the walls of Jerusalem. The Holy Lord suffered with the curses of death and the Power of darkness in order to make You free, the Child of the Holy Lord the once who is born of the Holy God. The Holy Lord is the Lord who makes history in your Life and the Life of the world.

As, the angel of the Holy Lord visited Holy Mary and Abram and told them a good news of the Holy Lord. Mary found favor in the Presence of the Holy Lord to give a birth to the Holy Promise Child the one who is Born of the Holy Spirit. The Holy divine God made history in their Life and the Life of the world. Dear friends if You don't know this God? come to Jesus he will change Your Life and make history in your Life, Just like Mary and Abram. Come to him, he will save Your Life from the curses of death and the Power of the darkness of the world to his Holy mountains. He will make You like some one who does history Like Moses and Paul. The Holy Lord glory and Miracle and Mercy will reveal through you and by your hands. The Holy Lord is the God who does history, he is the God who does history in your land, in the land of Christian nations and Your Churches. Throughout history the Holy Lord is known for his making histor. He will make history in America and around the world. The Holy Lord made history saving the world through Jesus Christ the Holy Lord gave Life to the Life of the world again. He is the faithful God who does history in your Church, family and in your works. You have to learn how to trust the Holy divine God who appeared to You and called You. God is the God who will help You to make history. Just, like he did through Moses, Paul and other disciples. The Holy Lord coming down to us, is the history of the Holy God and the history of the Lord's people. The Holy Lord will do history for you and through You. The Holy divine God is a God of history, he will do history in your Life and generations yet to come. As, I said, the saving, healing, guiding and Blessing works of the Holy Lord is the history of the Holy Lord and the history of God's people. My friends, the divine Holy Lord is with You, trust the God who called You, as the Holy Lord said to Jeremiah before I formed You I knew You in your mother womb and appointed You, set you apart as a Prophet for a nations. Jeremiah 1:1:6). NRSV. The Holy Lord knowing You and forming You in in your mother womb set You a part to be who God called You t be is the history of the Holy God and Your history. You are the history of the divine Holy God. Making You and forming You in your mother womb is the history of the divine Holy God. The Holy God called You to make history in your Life and the Life of the world. My friends, keep the faith, the God who called You before You were born and formed You and Blessed You. Keep honoring the Holy Lord who is merciful to You and Blessed You with long Life. The God who saved You from death. Keep Honoring the God who Blessed You and sends his Holy angels to watch over You and Your Family. The God who Protected from any kinds of accidents. Keep Honoring and Loving the God who give You a Job and good health. You are the Child of the divine Holy God, there is no great knowledge than these knowing the knowledge of the divine Holy Lord and knowing the Holy God is the

God who formed You in your mother womb before You were born. Don't think more than these or less than these. You are the Child of the promise, born of the divine Holy God. America, Christian nations, Church and Pastors keep honoring the God of Trinity the God who saved you from death and the God who saved you for eternity and transformed You. Keeping Honoring him and keep giving thanks to the Holy Lord all the times.

Give thanks to the Holy divine Lord, the God who made history to save you and transform the world throughout generations. Give thanks and Praise for the history of the Holy God, the God who come down and died for You and raised from the dead in order to make You his beloved Children's the once without the curses of death and the works of the devil but born of the Holy Trinity in the place's skull, Golgotha, the places of Christ suffering with the
darkness of the world in the hands of the devil. The places where the promised Child suffered for you and the Life of the world.

God Bless You and thank You very Much. Hope the Holy Lord Spoke to You.

UNDERTANDING THE HISTORY OF THE DIVINE HOLY GOD

The world is divided in religions, in languages and so many other things. For this reason, understanding the history of the divine Holy God and the history the Lord's people is important. The only way people can know the Truth is through understanding history. Understanding the history of the divine Holy God makes the Life of the world free. As, I said, in the beginning when the divine Holy God made the heavens and the earth and the mans of the ground in it. The Holy Lord revealed the Holy God own self to the Life of the world or the Holy Lord revealed the Holy Lord to the first mans of the ground. Genesis 3). NRSV.) When the Holy Lord made the mankind's of the ground, the Holy Lord gave them God's Holy Commandment to live according to the commandments of the Holy Lord, in the Presence of the Holy Lord. But the Holy bible says the mans of the ground did not kept the commandment of the Holy Lord. They broke the commandment of the Holy Lord and the curses of death, and the works of the devil entered into the life of the mans of the ground. The nature of the man kinds was afflicted by the nature of the devil. The Life of the world was fallen into the darkness of the world and the works of the nature of the devil. But, throughout history the divine Holy God was a faithful God with the Life of the world and the mans of the ground. When the mans of the ground fallen into the darkness of the world and the nature of the man kinds were afflicted by the nature of the devil the Holy Lord gave Hopes to the Life of the world and the mans of the ground. Since, the creations of the heavens and the earth and the mans of the ground the works of the Holy God continued throughout history of the world and human existence. From times to times the Holy Lord kept saving the Life of the world and the man kinds of the ground. The Holy Bible says the mans of the ground were swept away by the flood and Noah was a righteous person in the Presence of the Holy Lord and God saved him and his family from the flood. The Holy Lord gave Hopes to the world through Covenant with Noah. Genesis 8, 9,.) NRSV0. The first man of the ground failed to keep God's Promises and commandment. But, Noah was a righteous man in his generations and he found favor in the Presence of the Holy Lord. In the beginning of all things, the History of the divine Holy God was with the first man of the ground and with Noah. The divine Holy Lord appeared to Noah and the First man of the grounds and the story of the divine Holy God the God who made the heavens and the earth was with them. In order to understand the works of the divine Holy God throughout history is good understanding the history of the divine Holy God the God who made the heavens and the earth and the mans of the ground. The Holy divine God worked throughout history to save the Life of the world and the Life of the Lord's people. According to the Holy bible since the creations of the Life of the world to our world today, estimate the exitance of the mans of the ground can be about 20,000 years or more. Since the creations of the Life of the world the works of the Holy divine God continued throughout history. The Holy divine God saved the Life of the world and the Life of his people from the works of the devil and the darkness of the world from times to times. After Noah Covenant about after six, seven generation Later the Holy Lord appeared to Abram. The angel of the Holy God and the Holy Lord appeared to Abram and Spoke with the Holy Lord. The Holy Lord said to Abram When Abram was ninety-nine years the Lord appeared to him and said to him I am the God almighty walk before me and be blameless Genesis 1. NRSV). '' The divine Holy God the God who made the heavens and the earth made known God own self to Abram. The Holy Lord called Abram out of his country and relatives to the land, the Holy Lord was showed to him. The Holy Lord entered a Covenant with Abram to bless the nations through Abram. The Holy Lord said to him I will Bless those who Bless You and curse those who curses You. I will Guide You and I out of your spring I will make a great nation. The story of the divine Holy God the God who made the heavens and the earth was with Abram. The Covenant of the Holy Lord was with Abram, saving and transforming Covenant of the works of the divine Holy God. The Promises and Covenant of the Holy Lord was with Abram. The Holy Lord saw the life of the world through Abram and the Holy Lord called Abram to be Faithful to the divine Holy Lord who had called him. After Abram the story of the divine Holy God was with Isaac and Jacob. The Holy Lord appeared to them and spoke with them. The divine Holy Lord guided them. One of the things good to know is that these are the people, of the earth, first people who had Faith on the divine Holy God. The God who made the heavens and the earths. There are some other tribe the bible tells us that the hands of the Lord was with them, like Cush was known for their mighty hunters therefore they were known mighty hunters before the Lord. The Holy bible says in the first beginning of civilizations the mans of the ground started to built the tower of babel. After they started to built the Holy Lord come down to see the city and the tower mortal are built. When the holy Lord saw that the Holy Lord confused their languages, and they were scattered on the face of the earth. Genesis 11:1:9). NRSV.) Abram had two sons, Ishmael and Isaac. Ishmael was born of Hagar Egyptians salve. Isaac was the Promise Child the divine Holy Lord had promised to Abram and Sahara. Genesis 16). NRSV).

These is the first beginning of Civilizations. The mans of the ground were scattered on the face of the earth according to their speaking of langue's and tribe. As, I said, throughout history the divine Holy God appears and speaks to his people. Some other tribe of the earth get lost without knowing the God who created the heavens and the earth. They did not know the history of the divine Holy God the God who Spoke with first family of the ground, the God who spoke with Noah, Abram and Jacob. According to their own tribes and belonging they started to worship other gods. They started to follow certain types of people who were known as spiritual leaders of their community. But the divine Holy works of the Holy God throughout history is making another man kinds who did not knew the curses of death and the nature of the devil but born of the Holy God through faith in the Garden of Eden again. The divine Holy Lord was making known his divine works to all people who were scattered on the face of the earth. The Promise and the Covenant of the Holy God was saving and transforming the Life of the world from the curses

of death and power of the devil into the Presence of the Holy God.

After the Lord's people remained in the land of Egypt for almost more

than 400 years and they were suffered and cried out to the Lord. The

Holy bible says the Holy Lord saw their suffering and the divine

Holy Lord remembered his Holy Covenant and Promises with Abram,

Isaac and Jacob and come down to save them. To this time the only

religion or Faith that exists were the Faith of the God of Abram,

Isaac and Jacob. But, some other tribes they had their spiritual or

Faith leaders from their Community. They had their own gods they

believed in. On the face of the earth the only Faith that believed

into the divine Holy God the God who made the heavens and the

earth and the mans of the ground is the God who appeared into the

first family of the ground, Abram, Isaac and Jacob. There was no

Christianity, there was no Islamic religions and others. The only Faith

exists on the face of the earth was the God who spoke with Noah,

Abram, Isaac and Jacob. The God who made the heavens and the

earth and the mans of the ground were Promised in the beginning

to speak with all people, appeared to all people and makes all people

the Children's of the divine Holy God, the once who did not knew the

curses of death and the works of the devil but born of the Holy God

through the works of the Holy spirit in the Garden of Eden gain.

In order to understand the works of the divine Holy God and the divine Holy God who made the heavens and the earth, its very important understanding the history of the Holy God. As, I said, these divine Holy God, the God who made the heavens and the earth existed before even times and space. The divine Holy God was there in the beginning of all things. The divine Holy God was surrounded by his divine Holy angles and worshiped God. One of the things we understand the divine Holy God and God divine's Holy work is through the story of the Holy bible. The people of the Holy Lord wrote the history of the divine Holy God and the works of the divine Holy God for us. The wrote the history of the divine Holy God, the God who appeared and spoke with them. The wrote the history of the God who made known himself and his divine Holy works to them.

(I Read many religions books including (quran) the book of Quran they a Copied some of the story from   our Holy bible. The book of Quran is written in Arabic Languages there is also English translations. The way the books of Quran was written is, like a book of Prayers. Its only one book which means its doesn't have like Genesis, Exoduses things Like that. The way they wrote the story that is in our Holy bible, they wrote from the first Chapter of of the book of Quran to 114 Chapter of the book of Quran, which means straight, one one Chapter., 114). Most of its all the story of the Hebrew Bible and some of the New testament about the Birth of Our Lord Jesus Christ, the Birth of John the Baptist From Elizabeth and Zechariah. Its also talk about the story of Moses, Abram, Joseph and other Prophets. Mostly its about Prayers for the Mercy of god and they believed Muhamad is the last Prophets of god. When they believed Jesus the Prophets of God. One of the things I want you to understand is that Muhamed is the only Prophets from the that side of the people. The only Prophets who thought of different kinds of believes on those days. When all the Prophets, Moses, Abram, Joshua and other prophets of the Holy Bible teaches and confess about their Faith in the same knowledge and the same Divine Holy God the God who made the heavens and the earth. Mohamed was the only one who claimed to be a Prophets by recasting the same story of God, the God who Appeared to Moses, Abram, Jacob and Holy Mary. But he, claimed to be the last Prophets, when he supposed believe the dying and raising of the Holy Lord the one who was born of the Holy Mary through the works of the Holy Spirit in order to reconcile the heavens and the earth together. If he was true Prophets, he supposed to teach and being Baptized by the Baptism of John the Baptist. He supposed to claim the Holy Spirit was the one whom the Holy Lord was born from was indeed the third person of the Holy Trinity. They supposed to believed Confess that the works of the Holy God, the God who made the heavens and the earth was revealed to as through the works of the Holy Spirit through the Life of Jesus Christ. Since the story and the works of the Holy Spirit and Holy Mary and Our Lord saver Jesus Christ was written in their Quran. But, they denied the truth of God and the works of the Holy God. The mercy of the divine Holy God was only revealed through the suffering and dying and raising of the Holy Christ. The divine Holy God fulfilled his Promise to Abram, Noah, the firs family of the ground, Moses and all the works of the Prophets through the works of the Holy Spirit the one who proceeded from the Father in Whom the Father and the Holy Promise Child of God Jesus was worshiped. The divine works of the Holy God reconciling the heavens and the earth together were fulfilled through the works of the Holy Spirit in the Life of Jesus Christ, so that whoever believed in him and received him they might become the Children's of God and the Prophets of the divine Holy Lord.

Therefore, dear brothers and sisters, the teaching of one Person and the knowledge of one Person makes them a true teacher of the Faith or false, Prophets, teacher of Faith. Before there was Islam and Christianity the only Faith that believed in the God who made the heavens and the earth was Judaism. That was the faith that existed in the beginning. The God who Appeared to Noah, Abram, Jacob and

Moses. As, I said, Christianity is the Fulfillments of the Promises of the divine Holy God the God who Appeared to Abram, Moses and Jacob. The Holy Lord fulfilled his Promises in the Life of the Lord's people and the synagogues. When Jesus was born and started to teach and Preach in the synagogues and other places, the Jewish Community and the synagogues divided into two Places. Some people believed Jesus was the Messiah of God the one the divine Holy Lord had Spoken through the mouth of his Holy Prophets, promised to David and God's people that God own self will come and dwelt among them and they will be his people and he would be their God. Then the Christian Faith was started through the teaching of and dying and raising of the Holy Christ. After Christianity, for the first time Muhamad appeared to be claimed he is also a Prophets and started to teach the Islamic faith. Before that there was no Called Islamic Faith on the earth. As, I said, the teaching of Muhamad is the only different teaching in the history of Judaism and only Prophets from Arab family tree. That is why the teaching of him is not accepted in Judaism or Christianity.

The works of the divine Holy God entered the Life of the world through the works of the Holy Baptism. The divine Holy God, the God who was at work throughout history making the Holy Children's of the Holy God of the family trees of the earth was through reclaiming them through the fulfilment of the works of the Holy Spirit in the Life of Jesus Christ and Holy Baptism they all become the Children's of the Holy God. The once who did not knew the Curses of death, and the works of the devil but born of the Holy God through the suffering of the Holy Trinity a places of Skull, the places of Suffering. The Holy divine God, the God who made the mans of the ground reconciled the souls of the mans of the ground to himself through the works of the Holy Spirit in the Life and dying, suffering and raising from the dead of the Holy Christ. The Holy divine God reconciled the souls of the mans of the ground to himself.

As, I said, throughout history the divine Holy God speaks through many means. 1) The divine Holy God appeared and spoke to the first family of the ground the Holy God had made them. 2). The divine Holy God appeared and spoke with Noah's, Abram and Jacob and entered a Promises and Covenant with them. 3) The divine Holy God spoke through his Holy angels and sometimes dreams and visions. 4) The divine Holy God raised a Prophets and spoke to his people and the Life of the world through the Holy Spirit by the mouth of the Prophets. 5) As, the divine Holy God promised to his people, the Promises Child would be born of the virgin Holy Mary by the power of the Holy Spirit and the divine Holy Lord would, and will reconcile the souls of the mans of the ground to God own self again through the suffering and dying and raising of the Holy Christ. The Holy Lord appeared and thought and Spoke with the Life the world through Christ. 6) The divine Holy God called the Life of his Churches and the disciples and teach and Spoke with the Life of the world and his people.

Therefore, brothers and sisters the divine words of the divine Holy God stand alone. The divine Holy God speaks his Holy words, and they are effectful in the Life of the world and heavenly places. When the divine Holy God appears and speaks the words of the divine Holy God saves, guides and transform the Life of the world. Throughout history the divine Holy God spoke through the Holy Spirit to the Life of his people and the world. The Holy Lord spoke to them to renew them, to give them hopes and future. The divine Holy God spoke with them to guide them to the Promise land, the Land where the Holy Lord was Promised Abram. In the beginning of all things the call of the divine Holy Lord was the call for all human beings to understand the works of the divine Holy Lord and understand the divine Holy God. The divine Holy Lord called the Life of the world in the beginning to understand the divine Holy God the God who made the heavens and the earths.

For understanding the Holy angels of the Holy Lord, and understanding the divine Holy God the God, sometimes speaks through the Holy Spirit by the mouth the Holy Prophets and sometimes the divine Holy God who revealed the divine Holy Lord to the Life of the world is understanding the History of the Holy God and understanding the divine Holy God, the God who made the heavens and the earth. For understanding the Promises, Covenants of the Holy God, to the Life of his people is understanding the history of the Holy God and understanding the works of the Holy God. For understanding the works of the Holy Prophets of the Holy Lord is understanding the Life of the Promise Child, the Holy Christ and understanding the works of the divine Holy God. The Promises and Covenant of the Holy Lord throughout history is with the Life of the Lord's people and the Life of the world. For understanding the history of the Lord's people and the call of the Holy Lord throughout history is understanding the works the Life of the Holy Christ and the Life of the Holy Christ.

For understanding the story of the creations of the divine Holy God and the fall of the first family of the ground is understanding the works of the Holy Prophets of the Holy Lord, and the Coming of the suffering Christ and dying from the death in order to, make You his Holy Children's the once who did not knew the curses of death and the power of the devil but born of the Holy God at the places of Skull or Golgotha. The Promises of Abram and the works of the Holy Prophets, the Holy Lord Promised Abram the Lord took Abram Outside and said "Look up at the sky and count the stars if indeed you can count them, then he said to him " So You shall of Spring be." And Abram believed the Lord the Holy Lord. Genesis 15:6.). The Holy Lord will gather all people from all over the earth shall be gathered to the mountain of the Holy Lord and the mountains of the Holy Lord shall be exalted above all mountains. Isaiah 2:2). NRSV.) Many people will come and say Let us go up to the mountain of the Holy Lord to the temple of the God of Jacob. He will teach us God's ways so that we might walk on path he will judge between the nations and will settle disputes for many peoples. They will beat their swords into plowshares and their spears into pruning hooks nations will not take up sword against nations, nor they will train for war anymore 4, 3). ''

As, I said, throughout history we know the history of the Holy God through the works of the divine Holy Lord and the works of the Holy Spirit. The divine Holy God fulfilled his divine Holy Promises in the Life of Jesus Christ. Jesus was the Fulfillment of the works of the Holy God in the Life of the world and heavenly places. The Holy Christ is the God of peace for all humankinds. The divine Holy

Lord reconciled the heavens and the earth through the Life of Jesus Christ. The divine Holy Lord called the entire human family of the ground to the divine Holy God the God who made the heavens and the earth through the works of the divine Holy Spirit, in which term we use the third person of the Holy Trinity through the Life of Jesus Christ to God own self again. That is the Fulfillment of the works of the Holy God throughout history. Making all mans kinds God's own Holy Children's again. The divine Holy God called them back to himself and keeping his Holy Promises and Covenant in Pure Holiness again. The divine Holy God called them back to his divine Holy works and Promises through the Life of the Holy Christ again. In the beginning of all things the Holy Christ was the hopes of the Life of the world in the beginning of all things, the Lord was the hopes of the Life of the synagogues and all the Life of the world. Christ was the Change maker of the Life of the temple and the Life of the world. In the beginning the Holy Christ was the Hopes of America and the Hopes of the Life of the world.

Therefore, brothers and sisters, understanding the Life of the Holy Christ and the works of the Holy Spirit through the Life of the Holy Christ is understanding the history of the Holy God and understanding God. Jesus said to them, anyone who has seen me has seen the Father how can You say show us the father.? John 14:9).

NRSV.) He also said to them If I make You free You would be Free indeed John 8:36). NRSV.). Jesus was the Promises only Child who was died and raised for the Life of the world in order for the Life of the world to be free from the curses of death and the Power of the devil. The darkness force crucified the Holy Messiah and buried him but the divine Holy God raised Jesus again from the dead and he was ascended to heavenly places with divine Holy God. Jesus was meant be away maker for all humankinds to the divine Holy God through his suffering and overcoming death. The Holy Christ sets free the Life of the world from the curses of death and the Power of the darkness of the devil through his suffering and made them the Holy Children's of Holy God, the once who did not knew the Curses of death and the Power of the devil but born of the Holy Christ through the call of the Holy Baptism. The Christian Faith believes and Confess its Faith and believes in the universal God the God who made the heavens and the earth and all man kinds in it. As, I said, throughout history the divine works of the Holy God the God who made the heavens and the earth was at work through the works of the Holy Spirit and fulfilled in the Life of the Holy Christ in order to make all human being the Children's of the Holy God, the once who did not knew the Curses of death and the power of the devil but born of the Holy God through the suffering and dying and raising of the Holy Christ by faith. For these reasons, in Christianity we use the name for the divine Holy God the God who made the heavens and the earth as three in one, God the father, God Son and the divine Holy Spirit one God Ameen. That is the works of the Holy God revealed to the man kinds of the ground from the beginning to the Hopes of all things. That is how the divine Holy God has been at works and will continue to save the Life of the world and transform them to the Hopes of all things, things In heaven and the earth. Which in another Faith they did not understand God and the divine Holy God works in these ways? The works of the divine Holy God is all man kinds of the ground to know him and understanding God. The God news of Jesus Christ to go all over the earth and be told. Understanding and believing that throughout history the divine Holy God is with his people and with us. The divine Holy God who called them and chosen them out of the darkness of the world to his Holy Mountain to live for the divine Holy God alone. Having Faith, into the suffering of the Holy Trinity, with curses of death and the Power of the Evil.

Dear friends as I said, the divine Holy God the God who made the heavens and the earth throughout   history with his people. The divine Holy Lord gave them victory in all things. The divine Holy Lord guided them in the wilderness and feed them in the wilderness. He made away for his people in the wilderness. The hands of the Holy God and the miracles of the Holy Lord performed in the meddle of God's people. The Glory of the Holy Lord and saving hands of the Holy Lord, guiding hands of the Holy Lord, performed in the middle of the Lord's people. The hands of the Holy God divided the red sea, in order for God's people to cross to the Promises land. The hands of the divine Holy God let them cross over Jordan river. The Glory of the Holy Lord come upon Jerusalem and the nations. The divine Holy Lord defeated the darkness force for his people and the Lord's people started to live freely. Throughout history the Promises and Covenant of the Holy Lord transformed and Changed the Life of the Lord's people. The people of the divine Holy Lord they become a blessings to a nations. The healing hands of the Holy Lord, the Blessings of hands of the Holy Lord was in the Life of the Holy Lord's people and the Life of the Christian nations. Therefore, brothers and sisters there is only one God. The God who made the heavens and the earth and all man's kinds of the ground. The God who appeared to his people throughout history. The God who spoke with them, the God who said I am the God who is almighty, there is no one beside me, I was there in the beginning of all things. The God who said to Moses I am who I am, '' the God of Abram and Jacob and Isaac. The God of angles and the God who spoke through the Holy Spirit by the mouth of his Holy Prophets. The God of Jesus Christ. The divine Holy God who worked through the works of the Holy Spirit, in the life of Jesus Christ. The God who defatted the works of the devil and the curses of death for You. The God who called You to the eternal Life, the Hopes of all things through the Life of the Holy Christ. The God of Holy Trinity. The God who revealed the divine Holy God own self in the divine Holy Spirit and divine Promise Child the Holy Christ.

Therefore, brothers and sisters I hope You understand my teaching on the history of the Holy God and understanding the history of the Holy God and the works of the Holy God throughout history. I hope you know now what to teach and how to teach to the world about Faith. I hope I equipped You with great knowledge for You to understand God and the works of the Holy God, in the Life of the world and heavenly places. I believe no one can confuses You of anything more than these. Be strong in your Faith I know the divine Holy God will bless You and guide You.

Throughout history of the world, the divine Holy God is the God who made history. The divine Holy God, the God who made You and all creations of the Life of the world is the history of the Holy God. The Holy God calling the Holy Christ through the Life of Mary, by being born of the Holy Spirit is the History of the Holy God and the History of the Life of the world. The divine Holy God calling the Life of the Christian Nations and the Life of the world is the History of the Holy God and the History of the Lord people. The divine Holy God reconciling all the Tribes of the Life of the world, through the Suffering of the Holy Christ is the History of the Holy God and the history of the Lord's people. The divine Holy God, reconciling the heavens and the earth through the suffering of the Holy Christ, is the history of the Holy God and the history of the Lord's people. The divine works of the Holy God, the God who made the heavens and the earth Fulfilling through the Life of the Holy Messiah, is the History of the Holy God and the history of the Lord's people.

Dear Brothers and sisters, you are the history of the Holy God. The divine Holy God made the Life of the world, to make a generational history, in the Life of the world and the Life of the Lord's people. The Holy Lord saving, you through the suffering of the Holy Christ, is the History of the Holy God is the history of God's people. The Holy God, transforming the Life of the world through the works of the Holy Prophets, fulfilling all things, in the Life of the Holy Christ is the history of the Holy God and the history of the Lord's people. The divine Holy God, saving You from the works of the devil, through the Life of the Holy Christ is the history of the Holy God and the history of the Lord's people. The divine Holy God called You to make You history in Your Life, just Like Abram and Sahara. Just Like, the Holy Lord, raised Lazarus from the dead. Just Like, the women, with the issues of Blood, for twelve years. She touched Jesus clothe and healed, just Like that, the Holy Lord will make history in Your Life. Luke 8:43). NRSV.) Just Like that the Holy Lord called You to make history in your Life. Believe the Holy Lord, he is the God of History, the God who makes history in all things. The Holy Lord will raise You from the dead and give You and New hopes. The Holy Lord will take You to himself when the times come. You have to believe and trust the Holy Christ. Through Your family tree the divine Holy God, called You to his kingdom, that why God. So, that You will know the divine Holy God through the Christ and remain with the Holy Lord. You are God's History brothers and sisters, the works of the divine Holy God works through You, throughout generations. You are the History of the Holy God, the God who made the heavens and the earth and that is all in it and Christ is Our saver and Lord in whom the divine works of the divine Holy God fulfilled in heavens and the earth.

The divine Holy God Bless You and be with You now and forever. Ameen.

LOVING GOD

Dear brothers and sisters, the Holy God is, the God who made the heavens and the earth, the divine Holy God, the God who made the man kinds of the ground and that is all in it. The divine Holy God called You, to Love the Holy Lord alone. In the beginning when the divine Holy God called the Life of the world, the divine Holy God called the Life of the world to Love the Holy God, the creator of the heavens and the earths. The divine nature of the divine Holy God is a nature of Loving God. In the beginning, when the divine Holy God, made the man's kinds of the ground, the divine Holy God, made them, out of God's great divine Love. The divine Holy God, called the Life of the world to a being, out of his great Love and the divine Holy God called the Life of the world to love the divine Holy God, who made them and called them to a being. As, I said, the divine Holy God the God who made the heavens and the earth, is a divine eternal God and these divine eternal God is at work throughout history, in the Life of the world and heavenly places.

I don't know where You are in Life, you can be poor or very rich, You can be famous or nobody knows You, it doesn't matter? The divine Holy God is the God who made all things, together, things in heavens and earth called You to Love God. The divine Holy God, called You, a generational calling, so that You can Love the divine, eternal Holy God and serve Him alone. The greatest thing You can do in Your Life is Loving the divine Holy God, the God who made the heavens and the earth. The divine Holy God, the God who made the heavens and the earth created the mans of the ground, so that they can Love him. When the Life of the world Loves the Holy divine God, they keep God's Holy Promises and Covenant in pure Holiness. In the beginning when the divine Holy God, the God who made the heavens and the earth called the mans of the ground, the Holy God called them, to Choose the divine Holy God, rather than the works of the devil and the darkness of the world. The Holy God called the man kinds of the ground to Love the divine Holy God, the God who made the heavens the earth. But, the Holy Bible says the first mans of the ground, did not kept God's Holy words and

Commandment and they become a short Glory of the Holy Lord. They did not Loved the Lord, their God. The divine Holy God chosen You to Love the divine Holy God alone.

The divine Holy God, the eternal God, the God who made the heavens and the earth by God's own nature the Holy God is a God of divine Love. The divine Holy Lord, the God who made the heavens and the earth Loved the man kinds of the Ground. The divine Holy God Called his people to Love the Holy God. After the Holy Divine God Appeared to Abram, the Holy Lord called Abram to walk Faithful with divine Holy Lord and Abram believed in the divine Holy Lord who Appeared to him and start walk with the Holy Lord by Faith. Abram started building a Places of worship for the Holy Lord, the Holy Lord who Appeared to Him. The divine Holy God called Abram to his divine Love and faithfulness. The divine Holy Lord showed Abram his divine Holy Mercy and his divine Faithfulness. The Holy Lord Kept his divine Holy Faithfulness and Mercy to his Children's, Children's.

After the Lord's people remained in the land of Egypt, 400 years and the Holy Lord called them, out through his servant Moses. The Holy Lord Called them to Love the Lord their God with all their Heart and with all your soul and with all your strength. Deuteronomy 6:5).

NRSV). The Holy Lord called them to Love the divine Holy God with all their heart and minds. The people of the Holy Lord started to fallow the Holy divine God. The God who called them out of suffering and the darkness of the world. The God who saved them from the works of the devil and the cures of death. But, throughout their journey the Lords people sometimes turn way from the Holy Lord and did Evil. The Holy Lord was Faithful with them, when they turned away from Loving the Holy Lord and fallowing the Holy Lord, the Holy Lord calls them back to his Promises and Covenant again, and again. The Holy Lord Loved David, a man after God's own heart, and David Loved the Holy Lord with all his heart and minds to fallow the Holy Lord. When David turn away from the Holy Lord, the Love of the divine Holy God, the holy Lord called him back to Loving the Holy Lord and Following the Holy Lord again and again.

Throughout their journey, the Love of the divine Holy God and the Faithfulness of the Holy God guided and protect his people. The Holy Lord Called his people out of the darkness of the world and to God Holy Places, to Loving the divine Holy God. The Love of the divine Holy God and the Faithfulness of the Holy God saved the Life of the Holy Lord people and the Life of the world, and the Holy Lord called the world to Love the God who loved them and Called them out of the darkness of the world and the cures of death. The divine

Holy Lord called them to Love the divine words of the Holy Lord and His Holy Presence. John 3:16). NRSV.) The Love of the Holy Divine God, the God who made the heavens and the earth revealed through the Life of Jesus Christ. The divine Holy God revealed his saving, reconciling works of God's divine works through the Life of Jesus Christ. The divine Holy God called the Life of the world to His divine Love through the Life of Jesus Christ. The divine Holy God, the God who made the heavens and the earth revealed his divine Holy Love through the Life of Jesus Christ. The divine Holy God called the Life of the world out of the darkness of the world and the works of the devil to the Presence of the Holy God and Loving the God who made the heavens and the earth that is all in it. The Love of the divine Holy God revealed through the suffering and dying and raising of the Holy Christ. The divine Holy God called the world to God's Holy kingdom and Love of the divine Holy Lord again.

The Holy Bible says, when Jesus finished breakfast, Jesus said to Simon Peter, Simon's son of John do You Love me More than these.? Simon Said to him yes Lord, You Know that I Love You." Jesus said to him fed my lams,". Jesus said to him a second time Simon son of John do You Love me.?" Simon Said to him, Yes Lord You know I Love You." John 21:15 NRSV.). My Dear Brothers and sisters, the divine Holy God called You to Love the Holy Christ. The Holy

Lord called Americans and the entire world to Love the Holy Christ. The divine Holy Lord want the world to know if the world Loves him. Americans, the Holy Divine God called You to Love the divine Holy God. David Said, I will sing of your steadfast love, o Lord, forever with my mouth, I will proclaim your Faithfulness, to all generations I declare that your steadfast love is established forever your faithfulness is firm as the heavens, you said I have made a covenant with my chosen one, I have sworn to my servant David, I will establish your descendent forever and build your throne for all generations. "Psalm 89.) NRSV.

The divine Holy Lord, called You to Keep his Holy words and love him. The Love of the divine Holy God and the faithfulness of the divine Holy Lord came to the Life of the world through the suffering of Christ. The Holy Lord called You to Love him and fallow him. The divine Holy Lord, called You to walk by Faith with him and trust in his saving, guiding works, and transforming works. The divine Holy Lord called You to see his divine Holy Glory. The divine Holy Lord, called You to see, the Holy Lord on his Holy Mountain. The divine Holy Lord called You on Sinai, mountain, the divine Holy Lord called You the Places, where the Holy Christ suffered for his people. The places where the Holy Christ suffered with the works of the Evil and the darkness of the world. The Holy Lord is the healer of the Life of the world and Americans. America, Europe, the Holy Lord will heal you and transform You, to his Holy Presence. America, Europe, Canada, Australia and the world the Holy Lord called You to Love the divine Holy Lord on his Holy Mountain. The mountain of God's Holy Glory. The places of the revelations of the Holy Trinity. The divine Holy Lord called You to Hopes on the Holy Lord and fallow me. The divine Holy God, who called You and Chosen You through Christ will Bless You and Keep You.

So, brothers and sisters the divine Holy God, the God who made the heavens and the earth called us to Love the Holy Christ. The divine Holy God, the God who made the heavens and the earth, the God, who spoke, with Moses, Abram and called us to Fallow the Holy Christ and Love alone. The Holy Christ, suffered for You, to Love the Holy Christ. The Holy Lord called You to Love the Holy Lord and honor him alone. The Holy Lord is with You and he Loves You and Care about You. He wants to Bless You and make You Great. He wants to Prosper You and Bless You with Joy and Happens. He wants to Guide You. He wants Your Children, Children to Love him and adore the Holy Lord alone. He wants Your Children, the Children to Follow him and keep the Holy Lord alone.

God Bless You and Keep You now and Forever. Ameen.

THE GOD OF CHANGE

The Holy Christian God is the God of Change, the Holy God who Changes all things in the Life of the world and heavenly places. Since, the creations of the world, the Christian Holy God is at work changing and making all things new in the Life of the world and heavenly places. The Holy God the creator of the earths the things that is in heavenly places is the God of Change. The Holy God changes all things, in the Life of the world and heavenly places. Throughout the calls of the Life of the world and the Lord's people from one of the greatest works of the Holy God is Changing the Life of the world and the Life of the Lord's people to the calls of the Holy God in the Life of the world and heavenly places. The Holy God saw the Life of the World in God own self. Before, the beginning of all things, the Holy God saw the Life of the World in God own self.

What the Holy God has saw in the beginning of all things in the Life of the world the greatness of the Holy God and the greatness of the Life of the Lord's people. The Holy God saw the greatness of the Life of the world in all things in the calls of the Holy God. Before, the beginnings of all things, the calls of the Holy Lord to the Life of the Lord's people is the call of greatness in all things.

After the fall of the first family of the ground. from the calls of the Holy God. The Holy Lord saw the greatness of the Holy God and the greatness of the Lord's people in the Life of the world. The call of the Holy God to the Life the world and the Life of the Lord's people is, the calls of the Holy God to his promises, the promises of the Holy God in all things into the Life of the world and heavenly places. As, I have said, before the world was God saw the Holy world, before the nations was, the Holy God saw nations. Before, the Christian nations was the Holy God saw the Christian nations. Before, the Christian Church was the Holy God saw the Christian Church. Before the fulfillments of the promises of the Holy God, the Holy God saw the Fulfillments of his promises. Before, the Holy God saw the Holiness of the Christian Churches and the Christian Life, the Holy God saw the Holiness of the Christian Life. Before, the Economy was, the Holy God saw the Economy of the world, before the science was, the Holy God saw the science of the world.

Throughout the calls of the Life of the world, things change in the Life of world from century, to century, time and seasons Changes them in all things. But, the Holy God who made the heavens and the earths never Changes. The words of the Holy God and the promises of the Holy God never Changes. The Covenants of the Holy God and the presence of the Holy God never changes. The call of the Holy God is a call of change. Before Noah saw the Holy God, the Holy Lord saw Noah's in middle of the world, before Abram saw, the Holy God, the Holy God saw Abram in middle of the world. Before, Jacob saw the Holy God , the Holy God saw Jacob in the middle of the world. When the Holy God saw them, in the middle of the world, the Holy God called them for Change. Form small things to great things, from where they were limited into their own community, and culture, to great brought world and to the Culture of the Holy God. From small thinking to big thinking, from small Economy to big Economy. The Holy God changed their names. From Abraham to Abraham. Genesis 17:5). From Jacob to Israel. The Holy God called them, to the calls of nations and the calls of salvations of the world. The Holy God saw the healing of the world, through them and the works of the Holy God through them. The Holy God saw the Life of the Churches though them and the Christian nations through them. The Holy God saw the Life of the world through them. The Call of the Holy God and the Covenants of the Holy God Changed them. The Holy God saw the future of the world through them. The Holy God saw the future of the Churches and the Economy of the world through them, and the Holy God called them to Change, the Change of the Holy God. The God who changes, from low things, to high things, from unhealth, things to health things. From small things to big things. From small crowd to big crowd. From small family to big family. From mourn life to joyful life. From the ways of the Devil to the ways of the Holy God. From darkness ways to light ways, to the light of Christ. From poverty ways to abundant life ways. From war ways to peace ways, the peace of the Holy God. The God who changes, the bad things into the good things. The God who feels the empty jars with, full of oil.   The God who called you to greatness. The Holy Lord who saw greatness through them.

The Christian Holy God is a rich God by God own existence, for the creations of the Holy God is the richness of the Holy God. The revelation of the Holy God is the richness of the Holy God and the Holy calls of the Holy God is the richness of the Holy God. The presence of the Holy God and the revelations of the words of the Holy God is the richness of the Holy God and the richness of the call of the Life of the Lord's people. For the knowledge of the Holy God is the richness of the Holy God and the richness of the Lord's people.

The word Change originally comes from Hebrew words and Greek words Chalaph (חָלַף) or Greek ἀλλάσσω Corinthians 15:51) Genesis 41:14).NRSV. Which translate means, being transform or made being new. The word of the Holy God transforms or makes all things new in the Life of the Lord's people and the Life of the world to the promises of the Holy God into the Life of the world and heavenly places. The presence of the Holy God and the promise of the Holy God transforms or makes the Life of the Lord's people and the Life of the world new as a new creations in the promise of the Holy God always. The Holy words of the Holy God and the revelations of the Holy God transform all things in the Life of the world and heavenly places. The Holy words of the Holy God transform the entire person of the persona into the promises of the Holy God. The words of the Holy God and the presence of the Holy God transform or makes new, the thinking and believes of the Life of the Lord's people and the Life of the world into the minds of the Holy God. The power of the faith and the power of the Christian Life is the promises of the Holy God and the words of the Holy God. The presence of the Holy God and the covenant of the Holy God is the power of the Christian faith and the power of the Christian Life. The Holy Change comes from the Holy God alone and the Change of God is the revelations of the Holy God in the promise of the Holy God. The Holy Lord Changed the Life of the world throughout history. The divine Holy God always called them to Change. The divine Holy God is the God of Changes. The Changes of the divine Holy God works through the Life of the man kinds of the ground. In order for the divine Holy God to Change the Life of the world, the divine Holy God has to Change humans and beings of the ground. Throughout history the divine Holy God, the God who made the heavens and the earths called the Life of the world to Change. After the Lord's people fallen from the call of God and from the words of the Holy God. The Holy God always calls them back to his Holy Promises and covenant from times to times. The divine Holy God called them back to his Holy Promises and Presence again and again. After the fall of the first family of the ground, the Holy Lord called Noah. The Holy Lord called Noah to Change. The Holy Lord called Noah and his Family to be Faithful to the Holy Lord. The divine Holy Lord come down through his Mercy to save the Life of the world and the Noah's family. The Holy Lord commanded Noah to make Ark, that they will be saved in it from the Flood and Noah Obeyed the Holy Lord. Genesis 9). NRSV). After Noah calls, after many generations, the Holy Lord Appeared to Abram and the Holy Lord called Abram to Faithful to the Holy Lord, and Abram believed in the God, who made the heavens and the earth the God who called him. The Holy Lord called him to faith, to believe in the God who made the heavens and the earths. The Holy Lord called him to Love the Holy Lord and walk   Faithful with the Holy Lord. The Holy Lord called him, to worship the Holy Lord alone. Genesis 12, NRSV). The divine Holy God, called Abram to be different. The Holy Lord saw greatness in Abram. The Holy Lord saw a Great nation and a great generation in Abram. The divine Holy God called him to believe in divine Holy God, the God who made the heaves and the earth and the mans of the ground. The Holy God called him to believe in the divine works of the Holy God.

The Changes of the Holy God works throughout generations. Throughout generations the divine Holy God is the God who Changes all things. When the divine Holy God calls the Life of the world, the Holy God calls them for divine Godly Changes. If God changes one generation, the divine holy Lord changes many generations. The call of Abram, Jacob and God's people Changed the Christian Life and the Christian nations. When the Holy Lord, changed Abram, Noah and the Lord's people the Holy Lord Changed the Christian nations. The works of the Holy God always calls his people and the Life of the world to Change. The divine Holy God calls them to his divine Promises and covenant, to keep God's holy Promises and covenant. The Holy Lord called them to walk faithfully with the divine Holy Lord. The Holy Lord called the Life of the world and the mans of the ground to be like the divine Holy Lord, the holy Lord called them to have faith and on the divine Holy Lord and obey the words of the Holy Lord. The Holy Lord called them to believe in the unbelievable and walk with the divine Holy Lord by Faith. The divine Holy Lord called them to Obey the divine Holy Lord and the words of the Holy Lord. The divine Holy Lord Called them to have faith on the Holy Lord and to trust the divine Holy Lord. The Holy Lord called, his people from Poverty to abundant, from lack of knowledge to great knowledge and the wisdom of the divine Holy Lord. The Holy Lord gave them skills to make all things works for them. The divine Holy Lord gave them Courage and Hopes to Hope on the Holy Lord. Throughout the Journey of the Lord's people with the Holy Lord, the Holy Lord called them to his Holy Changes. Sometimes the Changes of the Holy God, comes through the wisdom of the Holy God. Sometimes the changes of the Holy Lord come through the hard times. Sometimes comes through suffering and pain. But the divine Holy God is the God who was, is faithful to his people and the Life of the world, throughout history. When the divine Holy God called the Life of the world, the changes of the Holy God came to them from generations to generations. For the Blessings of the Holy God and Prosperity of the Holy Lord comes through knowing the holy Lord and obeying the Holy Lord.

Dear Friends, the divine Holy God called You to Change, for the divine Holy Lord. The Holy Lord called the Life of his people and the Life of the world to Change for the divine Holy God who had called them. The divine Holy God, called his people and the life of the world to Change. When then divine Holy Lord appeared and speaks to his people, the divine Holy Lord, appears to his to call them to Change. When the divine Holy God, come down and speaks to his people, the divine Holy God did not just come, he come down to Change all things, things in heavens and the earth. When the Holy Lord, come down the Holy Lord come down to Change all things. The divine Holy God come down to call them, to Change. When the Lord people suffered in the land of Egypt, the Holy Lord saw their suffering and come down to save the Life of his people. The Holy Lord come down to save them and deliver them from the works of the darkness of the world and the works of the Evil. The Holy bible says, the Holy Lord spoke with Moses out of burning up bush. The divine Holy God called Moses to his Holy Presence and the divine Holy Lord Spoke with Moses out of burning up bush. Exodus 3:1-14). NRSV). First the divine Holy God changed Moses. The Holy Lord called Moses to believe, the Holy Lord called Moses to believe in the divine Holy God, the God who made the heavens and the earth. The divine Holy God called Moses to believe in the God who appears and speaks out of the burning up bush. The Holy Lord Spoke Moses in a desert place, a Places of suffering. A Places where there is was nothing only Moses and his flock. A place where was hard to find any hopes, the divine Holy God spoke with Moses. The divine Holy God bring hopes and healing to his people in a desert places, a place of suffering and hard to find Hopes. The divine Holy God called Moses to Change, he called him to believe in the divine Holy Lord, the God who appears and speaks. The divine Holy God said, to Moses, I have seen the suffering of my people and the divine Holy Lord appeared to Moses to save his people. The divine Holy Lord, appeared to call his people to the New Promises land and the new hopes the Holy Lord had Promised to Abram, Isaac and Jacob. The Holy Lord called them to the New Promise land, the Places where they build the New City and New hopes on the promises of the Holy God and the covenant of the Holy Lord. Into the land where they would keep God's Promises and covenant in Pure Holiness. The Holy Lord called them to the lands where they would build their city and Economy according to the words of the holy Lord, by being obedient to the Holy Lord. The divine Holy Lord called them to New Places and the New lands, to the Holy Land. The divine Holy Lord called them to the new hopes and   the New churches, where they can worship the Holy Lord in freedom. The Holy Lord called them to the Land, where they will raise their Children's, Children's in the knowledge of the Holy God and in the Presence of the Holy God. The divine Holy Lord called his people out of the suffering and the darkness of the world to where they would, and will obey they Holy

Lord, the God who appears and called them. The divine Holy Lord
called them from the land, where they experienced sickness and
death to the land, where they can live freely in the Presence of the
Holy Lord. The divine Holy God called them to his holy presence
again. The divine Holy Lord called them to a new covenant and
New promises again.   The holy Lord called them, to the land
where they would and will build the New Economy and the New
churches again. The divine Holy Lord saved them, from the hands
of the darkness and the works of the evil and freed his people. The
divine Holy God called them, to where their Children's will know
the divine Holy God and serve him alone. The divine Holy Lord
appeared and breaks the curses of death and the works of the evil
from the Life of the Lord's people. The divine Holy Lord Appeared
and called his people to his Holy mountains. The divine Holy Lord
thought his people God's divine saving works, delivering works,
healing works and miracle works. The divine Holy God called
his people to the divine Holy faith, faith in the God who made the
heavens and the earth. The divine Holy God who appears and speaks.
The God who appears and saves, the God who appears and Guides.
The Changes of the divine Holy God come to the divine the Lord's
people. The Holy Lord brought Changes to the Life of the world and
the Lord's people. The divine Holy Lord called them, to the new
civilizations, to New Knowledge, where they can build the New

world and the new earth. For the blessings of the divine Holy God and the revelations of the divine Holy God came through the Change of the Holy God. The divine Holy God called his people to his Holy change. One of the things I want the world to understand is that, we live in the Presence of the Holy God. The heavens and the earth lives in the presence of the Holy God including all creations of the Life of the world. In the beginning of all things, the divine Holy God called the Life of the world and all creations to Live in the presence of the holy God. The Presences of the Holy God covers the heavens and the earths, and the Holy God called the man's kinds of the Ground to live in his Holy Presences.

As, I said, throughout history the Change of the Holy God is in all things. The Holy God Changed the Life of the world in all things. The Holy Lord Changed the Economy of the world, the Holy Lord Changed, the civilizations of the world. The Holy Lord Changed the leaderships of the world. From traditional leadership, like kingships to modern ways of leadership. The born of the Roman empire, the leadership of Colonization's to our modern time Democratic leadership. The Roman empire passed away, Colonization's area also passed away and we are in a time of Democratic leadership. From Judaism Faith, Christian faith Born and other religion lately. In these all are the Changes of the divine Holy God, when things comes and they pass way. The divine Holy God is the God who Called You for Change. The Holy Lord always called the Life of the world, for Changes. The Holy Lord called the Lord's people to the New Promises land out slavery . The divine Holy God called them, out of the darkness of the world to his Holy Presence. Throughout their Journey, when the Holy Lord people breaks God's Holy Commandment and Covenant, suffering, pains brakes into the life the Lord's people and the Holy Lord called them back to Keeping His Holy Commandment and Covenant in Pure Holiness again and again. When they experienced suffering, pain and death, the divine Holy God called the Lord's people to Change. When the walls of Jerusalem was destroyed and the Life of his people, the Holy Lord raised a prophets among them and called the Lord's people to Change. The divine Holy God called them back to his Holy Hopes again. Throughout history the divine Holy God is the God who changes all things and calls the Life of the world to Change. Throughout history the words of the Holy God and the presence of the Holy God Changes the Life of the world. The words of the divine Holy God Changes the Life of the world and the mans of the ground. The only thing that can Change the Life of the world and the human beings is the words of the Holy God and the Presence of the Holy God.

Throughout history the Life of the world and the human being had their own believes and Faith. One way or another whatever they believed and knew destroyed their Life and the Life of the world. You live by the knowledge that You know and the faith that You believe in. If You believe in anything, it has a Power to work on You. For these reasons, nothing can change the beliefs of the Life of the world, not science or doctors nothing can Change it, unless the divine Holy God, the God who made the heavens and the earth. The divine Holy God is the God who can Change Your beliefs, he is the divine God who Changes the entire Person of the Persona. The divine Holy God calls the entire the Life of the world, to his fullness of knowing the divine Holy God and living by his Holy knowledge and faith. The divine Holy God frees the Life of the world and the humans being from the curses of not knowing him worshiping other gods. Throughout history the divine Holy God calls them to knowing him and the divine Holy God calls them to Faith. Nehemiah 2:3,4. Jeremiah 8:5Isaiah 1:21-31). NRSV.) The Holy Lord called the Lord's people to his Holy changes through Moses. Moses has to taught the knowledge of the Holy Lord and the laws of the Holy Lord to the Lord's people. The Holy Lord thought them, about Prosperity and how to keep God's Holy words and Commandment. After Moses the Holy Lord, called Joshua who thought the knowledge of God's the Lord's people. The knowledge of the divine Holy God and the

Presence of the Holy God changed the Life of the Lord's people and their Children and Children's. Throughout the works of the Holy Spirit by the words of the Holy God, the Holy Lord called the Lord's people to Change, the divine Holy God called them to faith, for Faith Changes the world. The divine Holy God called them to Change, to believe in the works of the divine Holy God and the Holy Lord. The Prophets of the divine Holy God called the Life of the Lord's people and the Life of the world to change. Jeremiah 31:31, Haggai 1;2, Isaiah 2:1:5). NRSV.) The Holy Lord called the Life of his people and the Life of the world to his Holy Change. The divine Holy God brought hopes to the Life of the world and the Life of the Lord's people. The divine Holy God called them to his divine Holy Change. The divine Holy God called them to believe in the things that is yet come. As, the Holy Lord said to the Lord's people but now hear O Jacob my servant Israel whom I have Chosen, I will pour water on the thirty lands and stream on the dry ground I will pour my spirit upon your descendant and my blessings on your spiring, am about to do New things, now its spiring forth do you not perceive it, I will make away in the wilderness and river in the desert to give drink to my chosen people. Isaiah 43, 44.) NRSV.) The divine Holy God called the Lords people to believe in the divine Holy God, the God almighty. The Holy God who does all thing in heavens and the earths. The divine Holy God called the Lords people to build the

New Jerusalem and the New nations. The Holy God called, them to build the New temple and the Holy City. The divine Holy God give Hopes to the entire world to gather together the entire world as Holy nations. The divine Holy God Called the world out of their darkness to his Holy Promises and Holy Covenant. The Holy God called them out of doubt to believe in the works of the Holy God and the Promises of the Holy God. The Holy Lord Called the Life of the world and the Lord's people to Holiness again. The Holy Lord's Called them, to His Holy mountains a Places of the revelations of the divine Holy God. The Holy Lord called the Life of the world to life and hopes again, in Jesus Christ. The divine Holy God called the Life of the world to Hopes and Peace through the suffering of the Holy Christ again. The Holy God called the entire world out of the works of the Evil to the Kingdom of the Holy God again. The divine Holy God called the Life of the world to Change again through the Life of Jesus Christ. The Hopes of the divine Holy God and the changes of the divine Holy God, the God who made the heavens and the earth came to the world through the Life of Jesus Christ. America, Europeans, Australians, Canadians, Jerusalem and the world the divine Holy God called You to his Holy Change, through the Life of Jesus Christ. The divine Holy God called You to his Holy Change. The divine Holy God called the Life of the world to faith again. The divine Holy God called You to believe in the works of the

Holy God and the revelations of the divine Holy God. The Holy God brake the curses of the Life of the world through the suffering and raising of the Holy Christ. The Holy Lord called the New world and the New Church through the Life of the Holy Christ, the promises child. World the Holy God is calling you out of the darkness of the world to His Holy Presence through Christ. Americans, Europeans, Australians, Canadians and the Life of the world, the Holy God called You to Change. Whatever You experience in Life, the Holy Lord called You to Change You. The Holy Lord called You, to give You Hopes and Peace. The Holy Lord called You, to Keep God's Holy Commandments and promises. The Holy Lord called You to Keep the Holy Christ. The divine Holy God, the God who made the heavens and the earth called You to work Your work by Faith. The Holy Lord called You to believe the unbelievable just like Mary and Moses. Americas the Life of the world, the Holy God called You to believe in the divine Holy God and the works of the Holy God, through Christ. Americans the Holy Lord is Your helper and Blessing, he is Your Peace and joy. The Life of the world, the Holy Lord loved You and suffered for You, to call you to the kingdom of God out of the suffering of the world to his Holy Presence.

Americans, Europeans, Australians, and the Christian nations the Holy Lord is calling You to Change.? The divine Holy Lord calls

You to faith, again and again. The Holy Lord Called You to walk faithfully with Holy Lord. The divine Holy God called you to stand on the Evil and the works of the darkness of the world. The Holy God called the Life of the world and the Christian nations to be strong in the Holy divine God. The divine Holy God called You to change for the divine Holy God on his Holy mountain. The Holy God called You out of the darkness of the world and the works of the Evil. The Changes of the divine Holy God revealed through the Life of the Holy Christ. The divine Holy God called You to His divine holy change, that come to the world through the works of the Holy Trinity. The divine Holy God called You to Change a Holy Changes for the divine Holy God and for the Holy Christ alone. Through the Holy Christ the divine Holy God calls You out of the works of the darkness of the world on his Holy mountain every day. The divine Holy God called the Christian Churches and the Christian Nations to change for the Holy God. Americans, Europe, Australians, Canadians and the world the Holy God called You to Change for the divine Holy Trinity, the one who Suffered with You on the mountains of Golgotha. The divine Holy God calls the Life of the world and his people to his divine Holy change, for generational Change. The Changes of the Holy God is, Economically Changes, Civilizations Changes, Politically Changes and spiritually Changes and the divine Holy God calls You to these Holy divine Changes.

Unless You Changes Americans, Europeans, Canadians, and the Life of the world nothing is going to change. You have to Change for the divine Holy God who called You, through the suffering of the Holy Trinity. The divine Holy Christ called You to Change for him. The Holy Lord called to change for him on his Holy Mountain, the mountain of Sinai.

CHANGE IS COMING

The Holy Lord is at work in the Life of the Churches and the world. Fulfilling his promises and Covenant in the Life of the world and heavenly places. The Holy Christian God the God of Change is with you, the God who is willing to change all things in your Life and the Life of the world, is with you. The Holy Christian God is the God who makes history, on your life, he is the God who does miracle on your life. The God who will call you from little things to great things, from thinking little to thinking big. From where you are limited to brought big lands. The Christian God is a God of greatness in all things. The call of the Christian life is a call of greatness in all things. The promises of the Holy God and the Covenant of the Holy God is the covenants of greatness.

Throughout history the divine Holy God, the God who made the heavens and the earth is the God who Changes the Life of the world. The divine Holy God Changes, things from the heavens and the earths. The divine Holy God the God who made the heavens and the earth is the God, who Changes the Life of the world. Throughout history the Holy Lord, was the Lord who Changed the Life of the world and the mans of the ground in all things. The divine Holy God is the God, who Changes the Life of the world in all things. The divine Holy God, Changes the Life of the world. He Changed the mans of the ground and the Changes the Life of the world. The Holy God, the God who made the heavens and the earth called the Life of the world to Change. The Holy Lord called the Lord's people to Change. As, I say Change is not overnight work, it is a Process, maybe from one generation to another generations. The divine Holy God is calling You to Change.   The words of the divine Holy God is a Prophetic word, in the beginning the divine Holy God spoke about the beginning of all things and the Hopes of all things. The divine Holy God speaks about all things, things in heavens and the earth. The divine Holy God speaks to the Life of the world. The divine Holy God spoke about the future of the world and the future of the Lord's people.   Throughout history the Change of the divine Holy God come through the words of the Holy God. The divine Holy words of the Holy God brought Hopes and future to the Life of the world and the Life of the Lord's people. Throughout the call of the Lord's people, the Holy Lord called the Lord's people and the Life of the world to Change. The divine Holy God called them to his Holy Change. The divine Holy God is the God who called them to change. The Holy Lord called them, to His Holy divine generational Change. When the Holy Lord's people, experienced suffering, Poverty, pain and death, the Holy divine Lord called his People to his Holy Change and Holy divine hopes. The divine Holy God is a God of Change. The divine Holy God called the Life of the world to change. When the Holy Lord people suffered in the land of Egypt, the Holy God called them to Change. The divine Holy God called them out of the suffering of the world to Holy New Promises. Exodus 3). NRSV.)

The divine Holy God is the God who brings You hope and future. The divine Holy God is the God who restore You. The divine Holy God is the God who calls You to his Holy Presence. The Holy divine God calls You to His Holy Presences. Moses brought Hopes and future to the Lord's people. The Prophets of the Holy God brought Hopes and future to the Life of the world and the Holy Lord's people. All the Prophets of the Holy God, spoke to the Life of the world and the Lord's people Hopes and restorations of the Life of the world and the Life of the Lord's people. When Samaria's experienced famine and suffering. The Holy Lord had Mercy on them and brought them his Holy hopes. The Prophets Elisha brought them Hopes from the divine Holy God. The Holy Bible says, Hear the word of the Holy Lord, thus says the Lord, tomorrow about these times measure of Choice meal shall be sold for a shekel and two measures of barely for a shekel, at the gate of Samaria. Then the Captain on who's the king leaned said to the man of God, even if the Lord were to make to windows in the sky could such thing Happens, But the Man of God said "You shall see it with your own eyes but You shall not eat from it. 2 Kings 7.)NRSV. In the land where people were suffering and Hopeless, the Holy God brought them Hopes and Life again. When the wall of Jerusalem was destroyed and the Life of the people, the Holy Lord brought them hopes and the restorations of the Life of his people and the Life of their hopes. Through the call of the prophets, the Holy God called the Life of his people to rebuild the Holy City and the Life of the temple again. After the works of the prophets, the Holy God called the Life of the world, through John the Baptist. The Holy bible says, in those days john the Baptist appeared in the wilderness of Judea proclaiming, repent for the kingdom of heaven has come near. "Matthew 3:).NRSV.) John the Baptist witnessed to the coming of the kingdom of the Holy God through the Life of the Holy Messiah. The divine Holy God called the Life of the world, to the works of the

Holy divine God, in the Life of Jesus Christ. The divine Holy God
called the Life of the world to change, and the holy Lord fulfilled
his divine Holy works in the Life of the Holy Christ. The Hopes of
the Holy God and saving works of the Holy God come to the Life of
the world and to your Life through the Life of the Holy Christ. The
divine Change of the divine Holy God come to the Life of the world
through the Life of the Holy Christ. The divine Holy God Changed
the heavens and the earth through the Life of the Holy Christ.
America, Europe and the Life of the world, God is the God who
Changed the Life of the world and Your Life.

The divine Holy God, the God who made the heavens and the earth,
God's divine Holy Change come to the Life of the world through
the Life of the Holy Christ. The divine Holy God has to Change,
the heavens and the earth through the Life of the holy Christ. The
divine Holy God has to Holyfied the Life of the world and the life
of the Lord's people through the Life of the Holy Christ. The divine
words of the Holy God has a Power to work in heavens and the
earths. The words of the Holy God brakes the curses of the world
and heal the Life of the world. The divine Holy God, the God who
made the heavens and the earth and the mans of the ground, saved
the mans of the ground from the works of the devil and the curses of
sins. The divine Holy God, the God who spoke through the Prophets,

Called the Life of the world to His holy Presence through the Life

of the Holy Christ again. What the prophets of the divine Holy God

had Spoken in the beginning, fulfilled in the Life of the Holy Christ.

The divine Holy God reconciled the heavens and the earth through

the suffering of the Holy Christ. The divine Holy God created the

New heavens and the New earth through the Life of the Holy Christ.

The Holy Lord said, to the Lord's people I am about to do something

New, now its spring forth do you do not perceive it, I will make away

in the wilderness and river in the desert." ISAIAH 19:21). NRSV.)

The Christian God is the God who make New things. He is the God

who makes away in the wilderness. He is the God who called You

to Bless You in all things. The Holy Lord Changed his disciples,

the Holy Lord called them to Faith, to believe in the works of the

divine Holy God through the Life of the Holy Christ. The Holy

Lord appeared to Paul and Changed him. The Holy bible says, while

Paul was on the ways of Damascus, Meanwhile Saul was still

breathing out murderous threats against the Lord's disciples, He

went to the high priest and asked him for a letters to the synagogues

in Damascus, so that if he found, any there who belonged to the way,

whether men or women, he as prisoners, to Jerusalem, as he neared

Damascus on his Journey, suddenly a light from heaven flashed

around him, he felt to the ground and heard a Voice say to him, Saul,

Saul why do You persecute me.? Who are You Lord Saul Asked."? I am Jesus who You are persecuting, Now get up and go into the city, and you will be told what you must do.? Act 9: 1:9). The divine Holy Lord called Paul to a change, from the works of the darkness to the works of the Holy God. The divine Holy God called him to his divine Holy changes. Through the Life of the Holy Christ, the Holy God the God who made the heavens and the earth Changed the Life of the world and the Life of his people. The God of the divine Holy changed the Life of the world, in all things. The Holy Lord changed the Life of the world Economically, Politically and Spiritually. The works of the divine Holy God is a works of Holy change. The Holy divine God changed the Life of the world in all things, from darkness to light, from Evil ways to Holy Christ, ways. From the works of the Evil to the works of the divine Holy God. The divine Holy God Changed the Life of the world. The divine Holy God called the Life of the world to Holy changes. The Holy Lord, called the Life of the world to Change, in Holy Christ. The Holy Lord called the Life of the world to Live for Christ, in Holy Christ.

Dear Christian's brothers and sisters, the Holy Lord, Called You to change. The Holy Lord called You to Change in the Holy Christ. The Holy Lord called the life of the world and the Christian nations to change in the Holy Lord. The divine Holy Lord called you to change. The Holy Lord Called Americans Europeans, Australians and the

Life of the world to change. The divine Holy Lord, called You to Live for the divine Holy God alone, through the Holy Christ. The Holy Lord called You out of the darkness of the world to Live for the Holy Lord alone, through the Holy Christ. My friends, you are the Chosen once of the Holy God, the Holy God Chosen you through Christ, to live for the Holy Lord alone. The divine Holy God called you out of the darkness of the world to Live for the divine Holy God alone. You are the one the Holy Christ suffered for You, on the mountain of Golgotha. The places of the Holy Christ Suffering for You. The divine Holy God Called you through the suffering and dying and raising of the Holy Christ to live for the Holy God on his Holy Mountain. The divine Holy Christ suffered with You and the darkness of the world in order to Change the Life of the world and Your Life. The divine Holy God called You to change for the Holy Christ. You are Chosen by Price by the surfing of the Holy Trinity. The divine Holy God is the God who always Changes the Life of the world and always Changes You. The divine Holy Trinity called You to change, for the works of the Holy Trinity. As, the Holy Lord changed his disciples and send them out to go and change the world. The divine Holy God also called You to change the world.

The Prophets of the Holy God, the lam of the Holy God Called the Life of the world to the Changes of the Holy God, that came to us through the suffering of the Holy Christ. In order to make the world and the Life of the man kinds of holy humankinds and Holy women the Holy Trinity suffered with you and the works of the darkness of the world and the force of Evil. The Holy Christ overcome of the works of the Evil and the curses of death in order to set You free from the works of the devil and the Curses of death. You are Free in Christ, the divine Holy Christ set You free in the Holy Christ. You are the changed one of the Holy God in the Holy Christ, the child of the Promise, the one who is born of the Holy God through the suffering of the Holy Trinity. The divine Holy Trinity set You free from the curses of the death and the works of the Evil. You are the chosen one of the Holy God, the God who appears and speaks. You are the changed one of the Holy God, the one whom the Holy Christ has Chosen.

Ameen.

THE MERCY OF GOD

Dear brothers and sisters, since the Holy Lord made the heavens and the earth and all man kinds in it. The divine Holy Lord looked the world, through his Holy Mercy. The divine Holy Lord called the Life of the world to his Holy Mercy again. When the Life of the world sinned against God and the words of the Holy God, the Holy Lord was angary against them. The Holy Lord judged them, with his angry. Throughout history, the Holy Lord called them back to his Holy Mercy again and again. According to the Holy bible, in the first history of creations, when the mans of the ground sinned against the Holy Lord and the words of the Holy Lord, the Holy Lord had Mercy and the mans of the ground through his Promises. The Holy Lord looked to the mans of the ground, through his Holy Promises and Mercy. The divine Holy Lord looked toward the world, through his Holy Mercy. When the man kinds of the ground turned away from the Holy Lord and toward darkness and the works of the Evil the Holy Lord saw the Life of the world through his Holy Mercy, through the call of Noah. The divine Holy God Called the Life of the world to his Holy Mercy. When the world turned away from the Holy Lord and followed the ways of darkness and overwhelmed by the force of the Evil, the Holy God called them back to his Holy Mercy and presence again and again.

After. the call of Noah, the divine Holy God called the Life of the world, through the call of Abram to his Holy Mercy and forgiveness. The divine Holy God calling Abram and entering a covenant with Abram is the call of the divine Mercy of the Holy God and the Covenant of the divine Holy God through his covenant with Abram and Noah. Genesis 18:2, Genesis 7:1). NRSV.) The Holy Lord called the Life of the world to his Holy Mercy through the call of Abram and Noah. The divine Holy God called them to his Holy Mercy. The divine Holy God said, to them, I am the God almighty, walk before me blamelessly." From times to times, when the Life of the world turned away from the Holy Lord, the Holy Lord call them back to his Holy Mercy again and again. The Holy divine God alone is, the only Hopes for the Life of the world and heavenly places. When they turned back from the Holy Lord and his Holy

Promises and did all evil, the divine Holy God called them back to His Holy Presence and Promises again and again. The divine Holy God said, to them I am Your Hope.

Throughout history, the divine Holy God, the God who made the heavens and the earth, kept his Holy Promises and Covenant with the Life of the world and Called the Life of the world to keep his Holy Promises and Covenants through his Mercy. After Abram, the Lord's people remained in the land of Egypt for 400 years. They forget the Lord their God. They forget his Holy Mercy and saving hands, of the Holy Lord, guiding hands of the Holy Lord. They forget, God's Holy Mercy and the miracle of the Holy Lord. The Holy bible says, God's people suffered in the land of Egypt, and they started to cry out to the Holy Lord. When the divine Holy God saw the suffering of his people, the holy bible says the divine Holy God remembered his Holy Covenant and Promises with Abram, Isaac and Jacob. Then he said, "I am the God of your father, the God of Abraham, the God of Isaac and the God of Jacob." At this, Moses hid his face, because he was afraid to look at God. The LORD said, "I have indeed seen the misery of my people in Egypt. I have heard them crying out because of their slave drivers, and I am concerned about their suffering. Exodus 3:1:7). NVI. The divine Holy Lord saw the suffering of his people and remembered his Promises and

Covenant Abram, Isaac and Jacob and come down to save his people. The divine Covenant and Promises of the Holy Lord is the Mercy of the Holy Lord. The divine Holy Lord is faithful to his people and to his Holy Covenant. When the Lord's people forget the Lord their God, God did not forget his Covenant and Promises with Abram. The divine Holy God, the God who made the heavens and the earths is the God of Covenant and Promises. The divine Holy God, Called the Life of the world and heavenly places back to his Covenant and Promises through his Holy Mercy. The divine Holy God called the Life of his people back to their Promises and Covenants through His Holy Mercy. The divine Holy God called them back to his Holy Promises and Covenant again and again. The force of the darkness of the world and the Evil have to leave the Life of the Lord's people, in order for them to be where the Holy Lord want them to be. The darkness force and the works of the Evil have given upon the Lord's people. The hands of the Holy Lord and the Merciless of the Holy Lord guided the Lord's people out of the land of the suffering into his Promises, Holy land.

After the Lord's people get into the Promise land, they turned away from the Holy Lord and they were attacked by the darkness of the world and want exile. The wall of Jerusalem was destroyed and the Life of the temple. When the Holy Lord Called the Lord's people out of the land of Egypt, the Holy Lord gave them a new ark of the Covenant and said to them, I will put my dwelling place among you, and I will not abhor you. I will walk among you and be your God, and you will be my people. Leviticus 26:12) NVI). The divine Holy God gave them a Promises that God own self would make his dwelling places among them and they would be his people and the divine Holy God would be their God. The divine Holy Lord saw the Life of the world and the reconciliation of the world, through the call of his people. The divine Holy God gave a Promise, to reconcile the Life of the world to God own self again, through the call of his people. The divine Holy God raised for his people who can speak to them the Hopes of the Holy God and the Mercy of the Holy God. Moses and the Prophets spoke with the Lord's people and the Life of the world the Mercy of God and the Forgiveness of the sins. The divine Holy God spoke to his people his Holy Mercy and reconciliations to the Holy God again and again. "I, even I, am he who blots out your transgressions, for my own sake, and remembers your sins no more. Isaiah 43:25 Hebrew 8:12 For I will forgive their wickedness and will remember their sins no more."

The forgiveness of the divine Holy God and the Mercy of the divine Holy God came into the Life of the world through the Life of the Holy Christ. The divine Holy God called the Life of the world and the humankinds to his Holy Mercy through the works of the Holy

Trinity. Throughout the call of the Life of the world, the divine Holy

God called the Life of the world to his Holy mercy again and again.

The divine Holy God called them through the call of the Prophets

and at the ends the divine Holy God made his dwelling places in the

Life of the world through the Promises Child the Holy Christ. The

divine Holy God, called the Life of the world, through the Life of

Jesus Christ. The divine Holy God called the Life of the world and

the humankinds to the Holy faith through the Life of the Holy Christ.

The divine Holy God called the Life of the world to his Holy Mercy

through the Life of Jesus Christ and the works of the Holy Spirit.

Now the Lord is the Spirit, and where the Spirit of the Lord is, there

is freedom. 2 Corinthians 3:17, NVI) the divine Holy God frees the

Life of the world from the curses of death and the power of sins and

give the Life of the world Hope and New Life again and again. The

divine Holy God called the Life of the world and heavenly places to

his divine Holy Mercy again and again. For faith in the works of the

Holy Trinity gives Hopes and Life to the world again and again. The

divine Mercy of the Holy God, the God who made the heavens and

the earth came through the suffering and dying raising of the Holy

Christ. The divine Holy   God called the Life of the world through

the Mercy of the Holy Christ. The divine Holy Christ suffered for

the Life of the world, his suffered with the works of the evil and the darkness of the world. The divine Holy Christ suffered with the works of the Evil and the darkness of the world and reconciled the Life of the world and the mans of the ground with the Holy God.

Throughout history the divine Holy God, the God who made the heavens and the earth did not take away his Holy Mercy from the Life of the world and the man kinds of the ground. Throughout history the Holy God called the Life of the world and the man kinds of the ground to his Holy Mercy again and again. The divine Holy God Called them, through Moses, through the Prophets, the Holy God called them through the Promises of the works of the Holy Trinity. The divine Holy God called the Life of the world and the man kinds of the ground to his divine eternal Holy Mercy. The divine Holy Lord called them through the suffering of the Holy Trinity, with the works of the darkness of the world and the Power of Evil, that separates the Life of the world and the humankinds from the divine eternal God.

Dear Brothers and sisters, the divine Holy Mercy of the Holy God which came to the world through the suffering of the Holy Trinity is sufficient for You. As Paul said in his writing But he said to me, "My grace is sufficient for you, for my power is made perfect in weakness." Therefore, I will boast all the more gladly about my weaknesses, so that Christ's power may rest on me. 2 Corinthians 12:9 NIV.) The divine Mercy of the Holy God and the Grace of the Holy God which came to us through the suffering and dying and raising of the Holy Christ sufficient for You and the Life of the world. The divine Holy God the God who made the heavens and the earth, the God of Jesus Christ called the Life of the world and the human kinds of the world to his Holy Mercy. The divine Holy Lord called You to his divine Holy Mercy form the works of the devil and the darkness of the world into the Presence of the Holy God and the Hopes of the Holy God. The Life of the world and Americans the Mercy of the divine Holy God which came to the world through the suffering of the Holy Trinity is sufficient for You. I will give you the keys of the kingdom of heaven. Whatever you bind on earth will be bound in heaven, and whatever you lose on earth will be loosed in heaven." If you forgive anyone's sins, their sins are forgiven; if you do not forgive them, they are not forgiven." John 20:23 Matthew 16:19 NIV.)

After the Holy divine God reconciled the heavens and the earth through the works of the Holy Trinity the works of the Holy Trinity continued through the call of the disciples. The divine Holy God called them through the works of the Holy Trinity, to proclaiming the forgiveness of sins and the divine Mercy of God through the suffering of the Holy Trinity from the works of the evil and the Force of the darkness of the world. Dear Brothers and sisters, the divine Mercy of the Holy God which came to the Life of the world through the Suffering of the Holy Trinity is for You. The divine Holy God loved You and suffered with You in order to set You free from the curses of death and the Power of the devil. The Holy Lord set You free from the darkness of the world and the curses of death.

Thank You and God Bless You.

THE GOD OF COURGE

The divine Holy God is, a God who saved the Life of the world.
God is the divine Holy God who created You and saved You. The
divine Holy God saved the Life of the world, from eternal works of
the devils into the Presence of the divine Holy God. The divine Holy
God saved You from the works of the devil. Throughout history the
most difficult things, is knowing the divine Holy God and its divine
Holy works. But, after the divine Holy God made the mans of the
ground, the Holy God called them to know the divine Holy God and
to know his divine Holy works. After, the divine Holy God, made the
heavens and the earth and the man kinds of the ground, the Holy God
called them to believe in the works of the divine Holy God and to
believe in the divine eternal God. Faith in the divine Holy God
Produce courage and Courage and faith in the divine Holy God the

God who made the heavens and the earth makes You live. In the beginning of all things, the divine Holy God, called the Life of the world to be courage's in the divine Holy Lord. The Christian Holy God is a God of Courage. The Holy Lord called You to be Courage's. Faith in the divine Holy God calls You always to be courage's in the Holy Lord. I don't know what You believe about Life but, Life has to be balanced. You have to have Faith on the divine Holy God, You have to work hard. You have to have time to enjoy Your Life and family Life. The courage of the divine Holy Lord helps You to live Your Faith ever day. The Courageous of the divine Holy Lord call You out of your bad early in the morning. The call of Courageous s makes You who God made You to be. The Holy Bible says, the divine Holy Lord says, to Joshua's, I will not fail you or forsake you be strong and courageous. Joshua 1:1;9). NRSV.).

The divine Holy Lord called You to be courageous. Life is a journey, from point A to Point B and its aps and down. But, through all You have to be strong and courage's in order to do what God called You to do. The courage's of the Holy Lord call You out of fear and doubt. The Courage's of the divine Holy God called You out of the darkness of the world to the mountain of the Holy Lord. Courage's in the divine Holy Lord calls You out of fear of the world to Have Faith on the divine Holy God. The divine Holy God called You to do the impossible possible and the courage's of the divine Holy Lord make You to do the impossible possible. You are Called to be courage's in the Holy Lord by faith. You don't have to take prescriptions in order to feel good about Yourself or to be strong. The divine Holy Lord is your strength. For Courage Produce Faith and strengthen in the Holy Lord. The divine Holy God called You to be with You in these Life and the Life that is yet to come. Throughout the journey of the Lord's people in wilderness to build the Promise land. The Holy Lord called them to be strong and courageous until they get into the Promises land. The Holy Lord, called them to be strong and courage's on the divine Holy God. The Holy Lord called them to build the Promises land. But, throughout their journey, they had a Challenge, until they get into the Promise land and build it. But the divine Holy Lord is a faithful Lord to his people, the Holy Lord helped his people. The hands of the Holy Lord made miracle for his people. One of the things I want You to all know is that nothing Happens without courage. You have to be strong and self-discipled in order to get done something. The divine Holy Lord is with You throughout the Journey, until You build Your Promise land. The divine Holy Lord, the God who keeps his Holy Covenant is with You. The divine Holy God called You to build the Promise land through You. The divine Holy God called You to be a leader like Joshua to lead the Lord's people to the Promise land and the Holy

Lord called You to be with You. You have to be strong and courage's to lead God's people to the Promise land, the land that is yet to come and the Promises land the earth that we live in. You are the Chosen one of the divine Holy Lord to lead God's people to build the Promise land. The divine Holy God called You to be righteous and righteous leader. The word Courage and faith stands together. The divine Holy God called You to live by Faith and courage.

The call of Courage makes You Live in the divine Holy Lord. The Lord who made the heavens and the earth. The Holy Bible says dived encourage himself to the divine Holy Lord. 1 Samuel 30:6). NRSV). The call of courage strengthens You into the Lord. Sometimes their will be a time You don't want Pray or do anything. On these days, Just Like David, You have to find courage and strengthen into the Holy Lord. The divine Holy Lord called You to have a bold faith on to the Holy Lord. The Faith that moves mountain and courage calls to bold Faith, to believe in the divine Holy Lord the God who made the heavens and the earth. Just, Like Mary said to the angle, nothing is impossible for God" Mary said I " am the Lord's servant Let it happen as you said." And the angel Left her." Luke 1:37NRSV.) The divine Holy God always call You to divine Holy faith. The Lord calls You to believe and faith gives You courage to believe the unlivable. The call of Courage call to the mountain of the Holy God. The call of Courage divided the red sea and the Jordan river. The call of Courage builds the Promise land. The call of Courage and the divine faith conquer the Life of the world and heavenly places. The call of Courage and Faith conquered the curses of Death and Power of the devil from the Life of the world and heavenly Places. The call of Courage and faith build the Life of the temple and the Promise land. The call of Courage and the divine Faith raised the dead from the dead and healed the sicks of the Life of the world.

The divine Holy God called You to be Courage's. One of the things I want teach You is, being Courage's in Christianity is the most important thing. In the beginning of all things, when the divine Holy God called the Life of the world, the Holy God called them to live by Faith alone. The divine Holy God called them to Trust in the divine Holy God. The divine Holy God Called them to trust the Holy Word of the divine Holy God. For faith into the words of the Holy God and into the Holy Lord makes You Live. The divine Holy God called You to live by faith and Courage in the Holy God alone. Faith in the divine Holy God makes You live, he makes You live in the divine Holy Lord. Faith and Courage call You out of the darkness of the world and doubt to believe in the divine Holy God. For faith and Courage build the Life of the world in Holiness in the divine

Holy Lord. Jesus called his disciples with him on the mountains, the
Holy bible says there he transfigured before them. His face shone
like the sun, and clothes became as white as light, there appeared
before them Moses and Elijah, talking with Jesus. Peter Said to him,
"Lord its good for as to be here. Matthew 17:1:18). NRSV). He
called them to the Place where the Glory of the Holy God raises on
the Life of the Holy Lord. He called them to believe in the miracle
of the divine Holy God and the works of the Holy God on the Life
of the Holy Lord. The Holy Lord called them to the Places where
the Glory of the Holy God shines on the Life of the Holy Christ.
The Places of the a Holy communion of Saints of the Holy God.
Throughout the Journey, of the Holy Christ, with his disciples, the
disciples overtaken by doubt and fear, from times to times. But, the
Holy Lord always call them out of doubt fear to believe in the works
of the Holy God and the Holy Lord again and again. The divine
Holy God calls them out of fear and doubt. The Holy bible tells
as on the day, when evening had come, he said to them, let as go
cross to the other side. And leaving the crowd behind, they took him
with them in the boats, were with them, just as he was. Other boats
were with him. A great windstorm arose, and the waves beat into
the boat, so that the boat already being swamped, but he was in the
stern of sleep on the cushion, and they woke him up and they said to
him, Teacher do You not care we are Perishing."? He woke Up and

rebuked the wind and to the Sea Peace Be still then the wind ceased there was dead calm." Mark 4:35-40).NRSV.). The divine Holy God called the Life of the world to believe in the divine Holy Lord and the works of the Holy God with all your heart and souls. The Holy Lord called You to rebuke the winds and the seas. The Holy Lord called the Life of the world to find Courage and Faith to rebuke the storm of Life, the winds and seas by Faith, by believing in the divine Holy God, the God who made the heavens and the earth, the God of Jesus Christ.

The divine Holy God called You to live by courage and Faith and Courage into the divine Holy God makes You Live. The divine Holy God called You to be courage into the divine Holy God and Live by faith into the divine Holy Eternity. Faith and Courage called You, out of the curses of death, the Power of the darkness of the world into the Promises of the Holy God into the Living Holy Christ. As, I said, the divine Holy God, called You to be Courage's and take heart in the Lord's by Faith. Sometimes You Just have to encourage, Yourself into the promises of the Holy Lord, and the works of the Holy God. Sometimes You Just have to give, thanks and Parise into the works of the Holy Lord, even when You don't feel it. Sometimes You have to remember, the wonders divine works of the Holy God and give thanks and Praise to the Holy Lord. You don't have to wait, until the divine Holy God, send his Holy angel and they speaks to You to give thanks and Praise to the Holy Lord. Sometimes the Holy God, don't tell You about everything in Life. You Just have to trust the Holy Lord and walk with him by Faith and Courage. Sometimes You just have to keep on Praying and Praising the divine Holy God, the God who made the heavens and the earth. You Just have to Parise the Holiness of the divine Holy God and His divine Holy Faithfulness to generations to generations. Sometimes You just have to Praise the wonderful works of the divine Holy God. You Just have to Praise him above all things else. The divine Holy God, God of Jesus Christ is, Your saver and Lord. He is Your guider and Your shepherd. Courge Into the Holy Lord and Faith call You out of the darkness of the world and doubt to the works of the divine Holy God and on his Holy Mountain. The divine Holy God calls You to God Holy Mountain out of the darkness of the world and self-doubt to believe in the divine Holy God and his Holy works. Courage and Faith makes all things works together, things in heavens and the earth. You have to be Courage's enough to pray every morning and at night that the Lord can do anything through You. The Blessings of the Holy Lord and the wisdom and knowledge of the divine Holy God comes through Courage into the divine Holy God and the Promises of the Holy God. The divine Holy Lord Called You to be Courage's in all things and the divine Holy Lord is the strength of the Christian Life and the Christian Church. The divine Holy God is the strength of the Christian nations and the Christian Churches.

David said, the Holy Lord is my strengthen and my shield my heart Trust in him and he helps me. My heart leaps for joy and with my song I praise him fortress of salvations for his anointed one. 28:7 NRSV). But, those who wait for the Lord shall renew their strength, they shall mount up with wings like eagles they shall run and not be weary they shall walk and not faint. ISIAH 40:31). NRSV). The divine Holy Lord is Our hopes, strength and courage. The Holy Lord renew the Christian Church and the Christian nations everyday day. The Presence of the divine Holy God and the word of the Holy God renews the Life of the Christian Life and the Christian nations. The words of the Holy God and the Presence of the divine Holy God brings Hopes and strengthen to the Christian Life and the Christian Nations. The words of the Holy God and the Presence of the Holy God brings Hopes to the Christian nations.

Throughout history the Holy Lord come down and speak to his people, the Holy divine Lord come down to give them Hopes and courage, the divine Holy Lord come down to guide his people in the right directions. The Holy Lord come down to guide them to the Promise land the land the Holy Lord had Promised to Abram and Isaac. The Holy Lord come down to call his people out of the suffering of the world to his Holy Mountain. The Holy Lord come down to save, and Holyfied his people. The divine Holy Lord come down to guide them to the Promises blessings. The divine Holy Lord come down to divide the red, sea and fed manna his people from heavens. The Holy Lord come down to anoint his people with the anointing of the Holy Spirit and the divine knowledge of the Holy God. The divine Holy Lord come down to destroy the wall of Jericho and the sins of his people. The divine Holy Lord come down to make the Life of the world his own people again. Genesis, 9, Genesis 17, Exodus 3,). The Holy Lord come down, to heal the land and his people.

Dear Brothers and sisters, faith into the divine Holy Lord made you courage. The divine Holy Lord is You strengthen and hope. Your Holy Lord is Your saver and Lord. The Holy Lord, Your Holy Mountain a place where You can hide. The Holy Lord is a Places of hopes and Joy for You a place where You souls rest in peace on the Holy Lord. The Holy Lord Called You be courageous in the Lord. The Holy Lord called You to do the impossible, possible. The Holy Lord is the courge of the Christian Life and the Christian Churches. The Holy Lord and the Presence of the Holy God is Your courge. The Holy Lord Called You to stand on the mountain of the divine Holy

God, by Faith. The Holy Lord called You to Bless You and prosper You. The Holy Lord is Your courge and hopes. He Called You to Bless You and guide You. You are the Hopes of the world. The Holy Lord called You to make You a Blessings to nations.

God Bless You.

Thank You

and God Bless You.